To Maria Farcas
from Hanna Ajami

MW01716286

Middle Eastern Cuisine

- Lebanon
- Syria
- Jordan
- Turkey
- Saudi Arabia
- Egypt

Sima Osman Yassine

Sadouf Kamal

Middle Eastern Cuisine

From the best selling cookbook

"Aleph Ba'a Al Tabkh"

Dar El-Ilm lil-Malayin

DAR EL-ILM LILMALAYIN

Mar Elias Road, Mazraa, Beyrouth
Tel: (+961 1) 30 66 66
Fax: (+961 1) 70 16 57
B.P. 11-1085
Beirut 2045 8402 Liban
e-mail: info@malayin.com
www.malayin.com

Fourth Edition
January 2003

Layout and Design By:
Samo Press Group

Printed By:
Phœnicia Press

Introduction

This concise book "Middle Eastern Cuisine" is based on the best-seller Arabic original "Alif Baa'a Altabikh" by the same authors. It conveys but a few of the common recipes that can be readily recognized by readers from outside this region.

Ever since creation, the Middle East was blessed with its geography, climate, and the variety of its natural resources, unique in their characteristics and quality. The peoples of this region had developed their blessings to an extent that ABRAHAM was directed to the heart of this region "The Land of Milk and Honey". A testimonial to the quality of produce.

Though many of these peoples were physically exterminated, their knowledge and achievements remained as our inheritance. The contents of this book should be a tribute to their meticulous efforts in the search and research for the identification of the ingredients, their values, tributes, their cultivation, and the methods of their usages, storage, and upkeep.

The dimension and domain of good taste and smell that these peoples must have achieved in their wholesome food and drink must have tempted the Romans into their ceremonies of good tasting.

Today the influence of other cultures and modern agricultural practices can be easily observed. Healthy natural products of this region as well as from abroad had given way to the scientific mass-production that narrowed the difference between products of different regions to the point of obliterating the original qualities and identity of the individual produce.

"Bully Beef" is an imitation of Middle Eastern Kawarmah.

Hard durable wheat of this region is still the best quality wheat from which the better biscuits and spaghetties of the world are made. From this wheat we derive Freekeh by roasting the wheat thistles, and Burghul by breaking the sun-dried, boiled wheat, both excellent substitutes for rice. The fine Burghul goes into many other recipes including Kibbeh and Tabbouleh.

Olives and olive oil of this region are still the best variety. Apart from being a wholesome meal itself, the oil is versatile in salads, cooking, frying and on its own as medication.

Sesame Seeds in baking and as a paste in sweets, and as a syrup in cooking and salads are also used as medication. Stuffed vine-leaves with the necessary side dishes for balanced healthy effect, cannot be ignored...

Contents

Appetizers 25
- Eggplant dip with Tahinah
- Stuffed eggplants in oil
- Fried eggplants with yoghurt
- Grilled Eggplants
- Swisschard stalks in tahinah sauce
- Chicory leaves in oil
- Pumkin Dip
- Green beans in oil
- Dried bean patties
- Stuffed swisschard leaves in oil
- Stuffed grape vine leaves in oil
- Fresh Fava Beans (lima Beans) in Oil
- Swisschard with fava beans
- Mana'eesh with cheese
- Mana'eesh with kishk
- Mana'eesh Dough
- Okra in oil
- Spicy raw Kibbeh
- Swisschard with blackeyed beans
- Shawarma
- Eggplants and Tomatoes in Oil
- Lamb spinal marrow
- Tahinah dip
- Parsley in tahinah sauce
- Tahinah dip with minced meat
- Stuffed green peppers in oil
- Minced green peppers with tomatoes
- Fried Kidneys

Salads 53
- Beetroot salad
- Beetroot and tahinah salad
- Swisschard stalks in yoghurt
- Carrot and radish salad
- Cabbage salad
- Cucumber and yoghurt salad
- Zucchini and Yoghurt Salad
- Fattoush
- Pomegranate salad
- Kidney bean salad
- Green Bean salad
- Lamb Tongue Salad

- All Vegetable salad
- Potato Salad
- Tabbouleh
- Tahinah Salad
- Green thyme salad (1)
- Green thyme salad (2)

Beverages 67
- Apricot drink
- Tamarind drink
- Karkadeh
- Liquorice drink
- Salep
- Turkish Coffee
- Yoghurt drink
- Cinnamon Tea
- Green Tea

Soups 75
- Wheat soup
- Cracked wheat soup
- Green wheat soup
- Bouillabaisse
- Rice soup
- Pumpkin soup
- Spinach soup
- Winter vegetable soup
- Chicken soup
- Yoghurt soup
- Lentil soup
- Chicken soup with semolina
- Tomato soup

Rice & Spaghetti 87
- Biryani rice
- Bokhari rice
- Fried carrots with rice
- Curried rice
- Rice with chicken
- Cooked Rice (1)
- Cooked Rice (2)
- Cooked Rice with Vermicelli
- Rice Cooked in Tomato Juice
- Rice with raisins and almonds
- Rice with Chicken and Yoghurt
- Rice with minced meat and nuts
- Shrimp and Rice in Tomato Sauce
- Spaghetti with chicken and White sauce
- Spaghetti with tomato sauce
- Spaghetti with yoghurt and garlic
- Spaghetti with Meat and White Sauce

Contents

Eggs 101
- Scrambled eggs with eggplants
- Scrambled eggs with potatoes
- Baked eggs in spinach
- Fried eggs with tomatoes
- Baked vegetable omelette
- Fried vegetable omelettes

Poultry 107
- Curried chicken
- Stuffed chicken
- Chicken with milk and rice
- Chicken with peas and rice
- Chicken with green pepper
- Chicken with rice
- Chicken in tomato sauce
- Spicy chicken
- Chicken with summac
- Chicken pie
- Yoghurt chicken
- Chicken in Yoghurt

Fish 119
- Fish balls
- Prawns with rice
- Baked spicy fish
- Fish steak
- Spicy fish with coriander
- Fried fish
- Fish with rice
- Baked sardines
- Baked fish steaks
- Baked fish with tahinah
- Fish stew

Vegetables 129
- Stuffed artichokes
- Artichokes with meat
- Stuffed pickled eggplants
- Baked stuffed eggplants in tomato sauce
- Stuffed eggplants with yoghurt
- Fried baked eggplants
- Fried eggplants

- Fried baked eggplants in white sauce
- Fried eggplants with rice
- Eggplant stew
- Lentils and eggplants in oil
- Swisschard with fava beans
- Stuffed Carrots
- Fried carrots with rice
- Walnut and chilli dip
- Fried cauliflower with rice
- Fried cauliflower
- Cauliflower stew
- Mashed pumpkin with burghul
- Fried pumpkin slices
- Colocasia (taro) with beef
- Stuffed cucumber
- Jew's mallow with chicken (1)
- Jew's mallow with chicken (2)
- Stuffed squash with tomates
- Stuffed zucchini in tomato sauce
- Stuffed zucchini in yoghurt
- Fried stuffed zucchini with lemon

- Fried stuffed zucchini in yoghurt
- Fried stuffed zucchini in tomato sauce
- Zucchini pulp in oil
- Stuffed swisschard leaves
- Zucchini stew
- Zucchini stew with yoghurt
- Green bean stew
- Green bean stew in tomato sauce
- Stuffed cabbage leaves
- Stuffed grape vine leaves
- Okra stew
- Dried okra stew
- Karbouzeh
- All vegetables stew
- Baked vegetables
- Stuffed turnips
- Baked stuffed potatoes
- Fried potatoes with coriander
- Sweet peppers in oil
- Spinach with minced meat
- Mashed potatoes with burghul(1)
- Mashed potatoes with burghul (2)
- Baked mashed potatoes
- Potato stew
- Stuffed tomatoes and green peppers
- Tomato stew
- Truffles with meat

Contents

Meat 173
- Stuffed lamb
- Stuffed lamb shoulder
- Chitterlings
- Meat on skewers
- Stuffed hearts
- Roast leg of lamb
- Meat balls with onions
- Baked ground meat in tahinah sauce
- Fried meat fingers
- Ground meat with boiled eggs
- Meat roll with boiled eggs
- Stuffed kibbi shells
- Kibbi shells in olive oil
- Mashed rice balls with meat
- Kibbi in tahinah sauce
- Kibbi shells in yoghurt
- Raw kibbi
- Baked kibbi
- Kibbi with sumac
- Kibbi with fava beans
- Lamb in yoghurt
- Stuffed neck of lamb
- Calfs feet with yoghurt
- Meat and yoghurt stew
- Broiled spleen
- Kabsah with meat
- Lamb fries
- Osso bucco
- Stuffed tripe
- Fried liver

Legumes 203
- Burghul with chickpeas
- Burghul in tomato sauce
- Green fava beans with rice
- Couscous
- Fava bean stew
- Pea stew with meat

- Boiled green peas
- Green hulled wheat stew
- Dried fava beans in oil
- Lima bean stew
- Kishk
- Lentils with swisschard
- Lentils with bread
- Lentils with onions and rice
- Lentils with onions and burghul
- Lentils with rice
- Pea stew in tomato sauce
- Chickpeas in yoghurt
- Chickpeas in oil
- Moughrabiyya

Pies and pastries 221
- Cheese pastry rolls
- Meat pastry rolls
- Spinach turnovers
- Cheese triangles
- Meat triangles
- Meat pancakes
- Meat pies in yoghurt
- Meat pie pastry
- Meat and pine nut pies

Desserts 231
- Dough balls in syrup
- Wheat in sweet sauce
- Pancakes with cream
- Cheese pancakes
- Kashta or home made cream -1-
- Kashta or home made cream -2-
- Walnut pastry
- Milk pudding with cornflour
- Milk pudding with cornstrach
- Milk pudding with sugar syrup
- Milk pudding with oranges
- Apricot paste with cornflour
- Plain rice pudding
- Milk and pastry pudding
- Caraway rice pudding
- Turmeric rice pudding
- Baked rice pudding
- Turmeric cake
- Semolina cake
- Semolina and date cake
- Pancake batter
- Walnut and date cookies
- Bread sweet
- String pastry with cheese
- Walnut pancakes
- String pastry with pistachio nuts
- Dried figs with nuts
- Quince preserves
- Apricot jam
- Date preserves

Basic Ingredients and Spices

General Information

Beans, Dried

All dried beans and peas - except lentils are soaked overnight before cooking. Soak in plenty of water with one teaspoon of soda. Change the water and place in a pressure cooker, (the water has to be 2 cms higher than the surface of beans). Cook for 30 minutes or until the beans are tender.

Burghul

Hulled wheat, cooked, dried then cracked finely or coarsely. Used in kibbi and tabouleh.

Cardamom

A necessary spice for Arabic Foods, sweets and coffee. The cardamom pods are ground and then used to give a better flavour for barbecue basting, sauces and cooking.

Coriander

Ground coriander seeds are used as a spice. Green coriander leaves are used in the cooking of stews.

Couscous

Couscous is the classic main meal in North Africa. It consists of fluffy grains of semolina, steamed over a rich stew of meat and vegetables.

Dill *(Shabat)*

This herb is greenish blue in color and has a slightly aniseed flavour. It is used mainly in Iraqi cooking.

Dried Limes *(Loomi)*

Dried limes are black limes that come from Oman and are used in the Gulf states, Iran and Iraq.

Fennel

This aromatic herb is called shomar in Arabic. It is fine, feathery and used a lot in salads.

Fenugreelk Seeds *(Hilbeh)*

These seeds are slightly bitter and are used in making pastrami.

Ghee

Pure butter fat. It is often substituted with clarified butter.

Gum Arabic *(Mistika)*

A resin from a small evergreen tree from Greece. It is used as chewing gum and also in cooking.

Harissa

It is a fiery condiment widely used in Morocco. It is made of hot red chillies, cayenne, olive oil and garlic, and has the consistency of mayonnaise.

Jews Mallow *(Melokhiya)*

Melokhiya is a plant native to Egypt. The leaves of Melokhiya are stripped from the stalks and washed then shredded. Melokhiya has the viscous properties of Okra. Dried melokhiya leaves are also available.

Kishk

Cracked wheat fermented with milk.
After it ferments it is salted and spread on a cloth to dry. Then it is ground finely and stored for use.

Mistika *(See Gum Arabic)*

Moughrabiyya

A cereal closely resembling Couscous.

Mahlab

This spice has a sweet fragrance and is made from the kernel of the black cherry stone. It is used to flavor sweets like Ma'amoul b'jaws.

Nutmeg

The hard inner kernel of the fruit of a tropical tree grown in the Far East and India.

For its full flavour, grind it fresh and try it not only in baked items, but in spinach or with veal.

Orange Blossom Water

A fragrant liquid distilled from orange blossom and used to flavour sweets and syrups.

Pomegranate Syrup *(rib rumman)*

This syrup is the sour juice of the pomegranate seeds combined with coarse salt and cooked over high heat. It is used in some salads and stews.

Purslane *(Ba'aleh)*

A green herb with fleshy leaves. The young leaves and tender tips are picked and used in salads and fattoush.

Rose Water

Distilled from fragrant rose petals, rose water is used in sweet dishes and desserts.

Salep *(Sahlab)*

A light colored powder from the tuber of the orchid species. It has a thickening quality similar to cornstarch. It is made into a hot beverage with milk and sugar.

Sesame Seeds, Black

Black sesame seeds or "habbat al Barakeh" in Arabic are small aromatic seeds used in yeast breads and cheese.

Sumac

The dried, crushed red berries of the sumac tree. Sumac is very sour and is used as a spice in meat stuffing and in making Za'atar (thyme mix).

Tahinah, Tahineh

An oily paste made from crushed, toasted sesame seeds. It is the main ingredient in hommos bitahinah.

Taro *(Ol'as)*

Taro or Colocasia is a large, starchy tuber with corms. Do not taste or eat uncooked as it is toxic when raw. Heating or cooking destroys its toxicity.

BASIC RECIPES

Beef Stock

- Peel the onion and carrot then wash with the celery and chop all the vegetables coarsely.
- Place 1 kg stewing beef and bones in a big pot and add 8 glasses of water. When the water comes to the boil remove the scum from the surface.
- Add the chopped vegetables, a bouquet garni, a teaspoon each of salt and allspice. Reduce the heat and cook-covered-for 2 hours over very low heat.
- Strain the stock.

6 cups

Chicken Stock

- Clean, draw and wash a chicken and place in a big pot with 8 cups of water. Bring to the boil and remove the scum from the surface.
- Peel and chop the onions and carrots coarsely.
- Add the chopped vegetables, bouquet garni, one teaspoon each salt and allspice to the chicken. Bring to the boil.
- Reduce the heat and cook, covered, over low heat for 2 hours. Strain.

6 cups

Vegetable Stock

- Sauté 1/2 cup of chopped onions in a big sauce-pan in two tablespoons butter or oil.
- Add 1/2 cup peeled, chopped carrots to the onions and sauté together.
- Stir in 1 cup chopped, peeled tomatoes and 1/4 cup chopped turnips and 2 cups chopped celery . Sauté all the vegetables together.
- Add enough water to cover the vegetables and bring to the boil over medium heat.
- Reduce the heat and cook- covered- for 1 hour or until the vegetables are soft.
- Strain the stock.

4 Cups

White Sauce
(Salsa Bayda)

2 tablespoons butter or margarine
2 tablespoons flour
1/2 teaspoon salt
a dash of pepper
1 cup milk

- Melt the butter over low heat. Stir in all the ingredients except the milk.
- Cook the sauce until bubbles form on its surface.
- Remove from the heat and stir in the milk.
- Return the sauce to the heat and cook until thick (2 minutes).

• • •

Garlic Sauce
(Salsat Toum)

5 garlic bulbs
3 tablespoons olive oil

- Place the garlic bulbs in aluminium foil. Cover well and bake in a hot oven for 30 minutes.
- When cool, remove the peel by pressing a little on the garlic cloves.
- Beat the garlic cloves with the oil and a little salt.
- Serve with grilled chicken.

• • •

Fish Sauce
(Salsat Samak Al Mishwi)

1 cup walnuts, finely chopped
1/2 cup oil
4 garlic cloves
2 cups fresh coriander, finely chopped
1/2 cup lemon juice
1 teaspoon salt
1/2 teaspoon red hot pepper

-Wash the chopped coriander well and drain.
-Crush the garlic with the salt, and sauté with the coriander in the oil until soft and tender
-Remove from the heat, add the chopped nuts, lemon juice and red hot pepper. Mix well.
-Serve with fish.

Pine Nut Sauce
(Salsat Taratour -1-)

1/2 cup pine nuts
1/2 teaspoon salt
1/2 cup lemon juice
1 slice french bread
3 garlic cloves

-Remove the crust and soak the slice of bread in a little water. Squeeze well and set aside.
-Crush the garlic with the salt.
-Crush or grind the pine nuts. Add the crushed garlic and the wet slice of bread. Mix well.
-Add the lemon juice to the above ingredients and mix well. Strain the mixture.
-If the mixture is very thick, add a little water or lemon juice.
-Serve with kibbi or fish.

• • •

Tahinah Sauce
(Salsat Taratour -2-)

1/2 cup Tahinah paste
1/2 cup lemon juice
1 clove garlic
1/2 teaspoon salt
1 tablespoon chopped parsley
Water

- Crush the garlic with the salt.
- Combine the tahinah paste with the garlic and lemon. Mix well.
- Add water, gradually, so as to make the consistency of taratour like that of mayonnaise or lighter.
- Garnish with parsley.

Makes 1 1/2 cups

• • •

Atter *(Sugar Syrup)*

5 cups sugar
1 1/2 cups water
1/2 teaspoon lemon juice
1/4 cup orange blossom water

- Dissolve sugar in water, stirring constantly.
- Bring to the boil, stirring occasionally, until syrup thickens slightly. Add the lemon juice.
- When the syrup is thick (10 minutes) add the orange blossom water.

4 cups

• • •

Bouquet Garni

A bouquet garni is a combination of fresh herbs that are tied together and placed in a piece of gauze then added to flavour soups, stews or stocks.

A bouquet garni contains thyme, parsley and bay leaf. You can add any herbs you like.

• • •

Clarified Butter

Is unsalted butter with the milk solids and water removed. It is prepared by slowly melting the butter so that the water evaporates and the solids fall to the bottom of the pan. The clarified butter is then either spooned out of the pan or slowly poured out leaving the solids behind.

• • •

Stuffing, Meat

To prepare the basic meat stuffing:

Peel two onions and chop finely.

Sauté the pine nuts in half a cup of butter, Remove.

Brown the onions and 400 grams of meat in the butter.

Season and cook for 15 minutes, stirring occasionally.

Remove from the heat and stir in the pine nuts.

Enough to stuff 1/2 kg of zucchini.

Yoghurt

To prepare yoghurt:

- Heat 2 lbs (1 kg) of milk until it is moderately hot.
- Beat a 1/2 cup of commercial or home-made yoghurt then add to the hot milk, stirring continuously.
- Pour in a saucepan and cover the saucepan with a lid.
- Cover the covered saucepan with a towel.
- Let stand for 4 hours or overnight without moving it.
- Keep in refrigerator.

To cook yoghurt (2 lbs or 1 kg of yoghurt):

- Crush a clove of garlic with 1/2 a teaspoon of salt.
- Add a few drops of vinegar to the garlic.
- Beat one egg and add to the crushed garlic mixture.
- Add 2 tablespoons of dissolved cornstarch in 1/2 a cup of water.
- Add the egg-garlic mixture to the yoghurt and beat well.
- Cook over low heat, stirring occasionally until it comes to the boil.
- Remove from the heat and use as desired.

Guide to weights and measures

1 teaspoon = 1/3 tablespoon

1 tablespoon = 3 teaspoons

2 tablespoons = 1 ounce (liquids)

4 tablespoons = 1/4 cup

8 tablespoons = 1/2 cup

16 tablespoons = 1 cup (8 oz)

2 cups = 1/2 liter

1 cup = 1/4 liter

1 ounce = 30 g

1 pound = 454 g

Oven temperatures

oven	electrical (F)	gas	centigrade (ºC)
Cool	225-250	0-1/2	107-121
Very slow	250-275	1/2-1	121-135
Slow	275-300	1-2	135-149
Very moderate	300-350	2-3	149-177
Moderate	375	3-4	190
Medium heat	400	5	204
Hot	425-450	6-7	218-233
Very hot	475-500	8-9	246-260

List of Ingredients

Allspice	(bahar)	بهار، بزار، فلفل أسود
Aniseed	(yansoun)	يانسون، أنيسون نافع
Artichoke	(ardichawki)	خرشوف، أرضي شوكي، إنجنار
Asparagus	(halyoun)	هليون
Avocado	(avokado)	أفوكادو
Basil	(habak)	حبق
Bean patties	(falafel)	فلافل، أم الفلافل، طعمية
Beet	(chamandar)	شمندر، شوندر، بنجر
Brains, lamb	(nkhâa)	نخاع
Bread	(khebez)	خبز، عيش
Cabbage	(malfouf)	ملفوف، لهنا
Caraway	(karawya)	كراوية
Cardamom	(hél)	حب الهيل، خاغ فولا
Carrot	(jazar)	جزر
Cauliflower	(karnabite)	زهرة، قرنبيط
Celery	(krafs)	كرافس
Chickpeas	(hommos)	حمّص
Chicory	(hindbeh)	هندباء، شكوريا، سريس
Cloves	(kebch kronfol)	كبش قرنفل، مسمار
Cinnamon	(kirfeh)	قرفة، دارجين، دارسين
Coconut	(jauzelhened)	جوز الهند
Colocasia, taro	(kilkas)	قلقاس، بطاطا قصبية
Coriander	(kezebra)	كزبرة، كسبر
Cornstarch	(nacha)	نشاء
Couscous	(kouskous)	كسكس
Cracked wheat	(bourghol)	برغل
Cream of tartar	(tartar)	مسحوق الترتار، الحامض الدُّردي
Cucumber	(khiar)	خيار
Cumin	(Kammoun)	كمّون، سنوت

List of Ingredients

Dried bean patties	(falafel)	فلافل، أم الفلافل، طعمية
Dried dates	(tamer)	تمر
Egg yolk	(safar albayd)	صفار البيض
Eggplant	(badinjane)	باذنجان، دنجال
Fava beans	(foul)	فول، باجلة
Fennel	(choumar)	شمّار، بسباس
Fenugreek	(hilbeh)	حلبة
Flour	(tihin)	طحين، دقيق
Garlic	(toum)	ثوم، تومة
Ginger	(zanjabil)	زنجبيل، سكنجبير
Grapes	(inab)	عنب
Green beans	(loubieh)	لوبيا، فاصوليا خضراء
Green hulled wheat	(frikeh)	فريكة
Green peas	(bazella)	بازيلا، بسلة، جلبانة
Green pepper	(fleyfleh)	فلفل أخضر، فليفلة
Jew's mallow	(mloukhieh)	ملوخية
Kidneys	(kalaweh)	كلاوي
Kidney beans	(fassoulia)	فاصوليا يابسة
Kohlrabi	(krimb)	كرنب
Laurel	(ghar)	غار (ورق)
Leek	(kourrate)	كرّات
Lemon	(hamod)	ليمون حامض
Lentils	(adas)	عدس، دال
Lettuce	(khas)	خس
Licorice	(sousse)	سوس، عرقسوس
Liver	(kebed)	كبد
Mallow	(khebbayzeh)	خبيزة
Marjoram	(mardakouch)	مردكوش، مردكوس، عطريشة
Melon	(chammam)	شمّام (بطيخ اصفر)

List of Ingredients

Mint	(nânâ)	نعناع
Mulberry	(toute)	توت
Mushroom	(fiter)	فطر، فقيع، فقّاع
Mustard	(khardal)	خردل
Nutmeg	(jawztettib)	جوزة الطيب
Okra	(bémié)	بامية، أوكرا
Olives	(zeytoun)	زيتون
Onion	(bassal)	بصل
Orange	(bourtoukal)	برتقال
Oregano	(zaatar barri)	صعتر برّي
Parsley	(bakdounes)	بقدونس
Pear	(njass)	إجاص، كمثري، عرموط
Pickles	(kabis)	مخلّل، كبيس، طرشي، مرقد
Pineapple	(ananas)	أناناس
Pine nuts	(snoubar)	صنوبر
Pistachios	(foustok halabi)	فستق حلبي
Pomegranate	(roummane)	رمّان
Potato	(batata)	بطاطا
Prune	(karassia)	قراصيا، خوخ حامض
Pumpkin	(yaktine)	يقطين
Radish	(fejel)	فجل
Raisins	(zbib)	زبيب
Rice	(roz)	أرزّ
Ridged cucumber	(makti)	قثاء، مقتي، فقوس
Rosemary	(iklil aljabal)	إكليل الجبل، حصا البان
Saffron	(osfor)	عصفر، زعفران
Sage	(kasiin)	قصعين، مريمية
Salt	(Meleh)	ملح
Semolina	(smide)	سميد

List of Ingredients

Sesame	(semsom)	سمسم، جلجلان
Sesame paste	(tahineh)	طحينة
Seville orange	(bousfeir)	بوصفير، صفير، أترنج
Shrimp	(kraydes)	قريدس، جمبري، ربيان
Shallots	(bassal ahmar)	بصل أحمر
Sodium bicarbonate	(karbounate)	كربونات
Spinach	(sabanekh)	سبانخ
Spleen	(tihal)	طحال
Squash	(koussa)	كوسى، شجر القرعة
Strawberry	(fréz)	فريز، فراولة، شليك
Sugar	(soukkar)	سكر
Sumac	(semmak)	سمّاق
Swisschard	(silek)	سلق
Tamarind	(tamarhindi)	تمر هندي، حُمَر
Tarragon	(tarkhoun)	طرخون
Thyme	(zaâtar)	صعتر، زعتر
Tomato	(banadourah)	بندورة، طماطم، ماطيشا، قوطة
Tripe	(krouch)	كروش، كرش
Truffles	(kima)	كمأة
Turmeric	(kourkom)	كركم، كركوب، عقدة صفرا، هرد
Turnip	(lefete)	لفت، شلغم
Vanilla	(vanilia)	فانيلا
Vine leaves	(warak inab)	ورق عنب
Walnut	(jaws)	جوز، عين الجمل، كرعاع
Watercress	(rachad)	رشاد، أبو خنجر
Yeast	(khamireh)	خميرة

Restaurant Guide

a la Carte: a menu term meaning "according to the menu".
a la king: served in a cream sauce with mushrooms with chicken or turkey.
a la mode: dessert with ice cream-or meat with vegetables.
Amandine: a dish prepared or garnished with almonds.
Antipasto: an Italian first course usually served cold.
au Gratin: a food coated with sauce and breadcrumbs and cheese them browned in the oven.
au Jus: served with natural meat juices.
Bisque: a rich cream soup frequently containing shellfish.
Blanquette: a white stew based on veal, lamb or chicken, enriched with cream, just before serving.
Bombe: a frozen pudding or ice cream in a dome- shaped mould.
Bouchée: a filled small pastry shell.
Bouillabaisse: a soup containing a combination of fish and shellfish.
Bourguignonne à la: cooked in a red wine sauce along with mushrooms and onions.
Cacciatore: food, usually chicken, prepared in a spicy tomato sauce.
Chasseur, à la: cooked with mushrooms, shallots and white wine.
Chiffonade: a garnish of julienne strips of vegetables, usually for soup or salad.
Croquette: chopped food in a thick sauce, shaped, coated with eggs and crumbs and often deep fried.
Croustade: hollowed out, fried, pastry shell used as a container for filling.
Crôute: a large piece of slightly dry bread, toasted, or browned in butter or oil.
Duchesse: seasoned mashed potatoes beaten with egg yolk and browned in the oven.
Florentine: a dish, usually egg or fish, with spinach.
Fricassée: a dish usually containing browned chicken cooked in a seasoned broth or sauce.
Jardinière à la: an accompaniment of fresh vegetables.
Julienne: match like pieces of fruit, meat or vegetables.
Lyonnaise: this indicates plenty of onions in the dish, usually fried.
Médaillon: a small round steak cut from the best end of a neck of lamb or a fillet of beef, tied round with a border of fat.
Mousseline: a dish with a small or large amount of whipped cream added.
En Papillote: food prepared, cooked and served in parchment, wax paper or aluminum foil.
Parmigiana: prepared using Parmesan cheese.
Pilaf, Pilau: an Indian rice dish served with curry.
Ragoût: a thick, highly seasoned stew.
Risotto: a dish made from Italian rice simmered in stock.
Roulade: a thin piece of meat, stuffed or not, rolled up and cooked.
Scallopini: usually refers to veal "pieces" or (scallops) of veal.
Scampi: Shrimp.
Tempura: a deep-fried Japanese fish or vegetable dish, for which a special tempura batter is used.
Torte: a kind of rich Austrian cake.
Tournedo: a slice of beef tenderloin about 1 inch thick.
Vinaigrette: a seasoned vinegar and oil sauce.

APPETIZERS

Eggplant Dip with Tahinah

Badinjan Bi tahina

2 lb (1 kg) eggplants
3 garlic cloves
1 tablespoon water
1/2 teaspoon salt
1/2 cup tahinah paste
(ground, hulled seame seeds)
Juice of one and a half lemons

5 persons

- ▼ Grill the eggplants then mash the pulp.
- ▼ Crush the garlic cloves with the salt in a pestle, then stir in the lemon juice.
- ▼ Add the above mixture to the mashed eggplants, then stir in the tahinah and water.
- ▼ Serve in a bowl and sprinkle with chopped parsley and a little cumin.

Stuffed Eggplants in Oil

Badinjan Mihshi b'zeit

2 lb (1 kg) small eggplants
2 medium-sized onions
3 large tomatoes
1 1/2 cups chopped parsley
1/2 cup short grain rice
1/2 cup olive oil
1 green pepper
a dash of black pepper
juice of 3 lemons

4 persons

- ▼ Chop the onions very finely and rub them with salt and pepper.
- ▼ Chop the tomatoes very finely, then wash the rice in several waters.
- ▼ Drain the rice and mix with the onions, tomatoes and parsley.
- ▼ Stir in the olive oil and the lemon juice.
- ▼ To make scooping out the eggplants easier, roll each eggplant between your hands for a while.
- ▼ Cut off the stem ends of the eggplants, then scoop out the pulp leaving a shell about 3/4 centimeter thick.
- ▼ Three-quarters fill the eggplants with the rice mixture allowing for rice expansion.
- ▼ Cut the green pepper into rings and arrange them at bottom of the saucepan.
- ▼ Place the stuffed eggplants over the pepper rings in closely packed rows and layers.
- ▼ Pour the sauce of the rice mixture plus one cup and a half of water over the eggplants.
- ▼ Sprinkle the eggplants with salt, then turn a dinner plate upside-down over the eggplants to keep them in place.
- ▼ Cover the saucepan, bring to the boil, then turn down the heat and allow to simmer for 2 hours.
- ▼ Allow to cool before turning on to the serving dish.

Fried Eggplants with Yoghurt
Badinjan Makli ma'a Laban

3 medium-sized eggplants (2 lb)
1 cup yoghurt
5 garlic cloves, peeled
a dash of salt
a dash of dried, crushed, mint leaves

2 persons

- Pare the eggplants and cut them into half-inch slices, then sprinkle them with salt and put them aside for a while.
- Drain the slices and fry them in oil until golden.
- Drain them on absorbent paper and place on a plate.
- Crush the garlic cloves in a pestle with the salt and dried mint, then stir them into the yoghurt.
- Pour the yoghurt mixture over the eggplant slices and serve.

Grilled Eggplants
Badinjan Mishwi

4 garlic cloves, peeled
2 tablespoons chopped parsley
(flat-leaf parsley is preferable)
1/2 teaspoon salt
3 medium-sized eggplants
(2 lb or 1 kg)

5 persons

- Roast the eggplants by placing each on a gas flame and turning it over the fire until the skin is charred and begins to split.
- When the eggplants are cool enough to handle, skin them and mash the pulp to a smooth purée.
- Crush the garlic cloves with the salt, (preferably in a pestle) and stir it into the mashed eggplants.
- Place the purée in a plate and sprinkle the top with olive oil and chopped parsley.

Swisschard Stalks in Tahinah Sauce

Silq Bi Tahinah

1 lb (1/2 kg) swisschard stalks
1/2 cup tahinah paste
5 garlic cloves
3/4 cup fresh lemon juice
1 teaspoon salt

5 persons

- ▼ Boil the stalks by placing them in two cups boiling water.
- ▼ Reduce heat cover and simmer until tender for about 20 minutes.
- ▼ Simmer until tender for about 20 minutes.
- ▼ Wash the stalks, then chop coarsely and drain.
- ▼ Crush the stalks in a pestle and mortar. Crush the garlic and stir in the salt, lemon juice and tahinah paste.
- ▼ Blend the above mixture well; pour into small platters.
- ▼ These platters are served with stuffed Swisschard leaves.

Chicory Leaves in Oil
Hindbeh b'Zeit

2 lb (1 kg) chicory
1/2 cup olive oil
3 onions, sliced into thin rings
1 tablespoon salt
5 garlic cloves

5 persons

- ▼ Remove the outer yellow leaves from the chicory, then wash and shred crosswise, very finely.
- ▼ Immerse the shredded leaves in hot water for 2 minutes.
- ▼ When almost tender, remove the leaves and squeeze out excess water between the palms of the hand.
- ▼ Set aside to cool.
- ▼ Fry the onion rings in oil until golden.
- ▼ Remove the onions from the oil and place the chicory in the same oil with the crushed garlic and salt.
- ▼ Sauté over medium heat for 15 minutes.
- ▼ Pour some lemon juice over it and serve cold, granished with the fried onion rings .

Pumpkin Dip
Qara'a bi Tahinah

2 lb (1 kg) pumpkin
1/2 cup lemon juice
4 garlic cloves
1/2 tablespoon salt
1/2 cup tahinah sauce (paste)
1/4 cup parsley, finely chopped

5 persons

▼ Peel, slice and remove the seeds from the pumpkin.

▼ Add one cup of water to the pumpkin slices and cook them, covered, over medium heat for 40 minutes.

▼ Drain the pumpkin well, then put it through a vegetable strainer.

▼ Add the tahinah to the pumpkin purée and stir well.

▼ Crush the garlic cloves with the salt well, then stir in the lemon juice.

▼ Add the garlic mixture to the pumpkin purée and stir well.

▼ Serve in small platters and sprinkle with a little amount of cumin and chopped parsley.

Green Beans in Oil

Lubyah b'Zeit

2 lb (1 kg) green beans
3 large onions, thinly sliced
6 garlic cloves
1/2 cup olive oil
3 lb (1 1/2 kg) ripe tomatoes, peeled and chopped
1 tablespoon salt
a dash of pepper

4 persons

- Snip off the ends, then string, wash and drain the beans well.
- Sauté the onions and garlic in the oil until light brown in color.
- Stir in the beans, salt and pepper and chopped tomatoes.
- Bring to the boil, then reduce the heat and let simmer for half an hour or until tender.
- Serve cold.
- It is preferable to add some crushed garlic cloves with dried mint to the beans, a few minutes before cooking is over.

Dried Bean Patties
Falafel

2 cups dried fava beans
1/2 cup chickpeas
3 whole garlic bulbs
3 onions
1/2 cup green coriander, finely copped
2 tablespoons parsley, finely chopped
1/4 cup bread crumbs
1 tablespoon salt
1 teaspoon pepper
1 teaspoon dried ground coriander
1/2 teaspoon powdered hot chilli
1/2 teaspoon black pepper
1/2 teaspoon powdered cumin
1/2 teaspoon cinnamon
1 teaspoon bicarbonate of soda
1 teaspoon baking powder
5 cups vegetable oil for frying

70 patties

▼ Soak both the fava beans and chickpeas in water overnight.

▼ Drain the fava beans and chickpeas.

▼ Peel the garlic and onions and chop finely.

▼ Mix all ingredients except the seasoning and put them through the meat grinder twice.

▼ Add the seasoning, bicarbonate of soda and baking powder to the above mixture and knead well with the hands.

▼ Leave the kneaded mixture aside for one hour and a half, then knead again.

▼ Wet the hands a little and take a tablespoon - sized piece of the mixture - one at a time - and shape into small round patties. (3 cms in diameter).

▼ Deep-fry in hot oil until golden brown.

▼ Serve hot, with cucumber salad and tahinah sauce.

Stuffed Swisschard Leaves in Oil

Mihshi Silq b' Zeit

2 lb (1 kg) fresh swisschard
3 cups chopped parsley
2 onions
1/2 cup olive oil
3 large ripe tomatoes
3/4 cup rice, washed in several waters
1 tablespoon salt
a few mint leaves
juice of 2 lemons
a dash of pepper

5 persons

- ▼ Chop the onions finely and rub with salt and pepper.
- ▼ Chop the tomatoes and the mint leaves very finely and place in a medium-size mixing bowl, then stir in the rice.
- ▼ Add the parsley, olive oil and lemon juice and mix well.
- ▼ Cut off the swisschard stems and wash the leaves well.
- ▼ Drop the leaves in boiling water for a few seconds then remove quickly.
- ▼ Stuff the leaves (see stuffed vine leaves).
- ▼ Place a few stalks at the bottom of a saucepan, then place the stuffed leaves over them in closely packed rows and layers.
- ▼ Pour the remaining sauce from the rice mixture and add enough water to cover the stuffed leaves. Turn a platter upside-down over the leaves to keep them in place.
- ▼ Cover the saucepan and bring to the boil. Reduce heat and simmer for an hour.
- ▼ When the leaves are almost cold, turn onto a plate and garnish with a few tomato rings.

Stuffed Grape Vine Leaves in Oil

Wara' Enab b'Zeit

6 oz (200 g) grape vine leaves
3 cups finely chopped parsley
3/4 cup short-grain rice, washed
3 large ripe tomatoes
1 cup olive oil
1/2 tablespoon salt
2 Bermuda (red) onions
1 potato
a dash of pepper
a few mint leaves
juice of 2 lemons

10 persons

- ▼ Chop the onions very finely, then rub them with salt and pepper.
- ▼ Chop the tomatoes very finely, then combine with the chopped parsley and chopped mint.
- ▼ Add the rice to the onions and tomatoes and parsley and mix very well.
- ▼ Stir in the olive oil and lemon juice, and set aside.
- ▼ Meanwhile, peel the potato and cut it into rounds and arrange them at the bottom of the saucepan.
- ▼ Cut off the stems from the leaves, then wash them.
- ▼ Drop the leaves-a few at a time-in boiling water then remove quickly.
- ▼ Place shiny side down on a board, then put one teaspoon of filling at the broad end of the leaf.
- ▼ Fold over the left and right segments, then roll the leaf from beyond the filling towards its tip.
- ▼ Place the rolls seam-end down, in tight rows and layers on top of the potato slices.
- ▼ Cover the layers of vine leaves with a plate turned upside-down, to keep them in place.
- ▼ Pour the remainder of the filling sauce and a cup of water on top of the leaves.
- ▼ Place the saucepan over medium heat until it starts boiling.
- ▼ Reduce the heat and let simmer for one hour.
- ▼ Serve cold garnished with tomato rings.

Fresh Fava Beans (Lima Beans) in Oil

Foul Akhdar b'Zeit

2 lb (1 kg) green fava beans
1/2 cup olive oil
5 onions finely chopped
1 teaspoon salt
1/2 cup water
1 cup chopped coriander
5 garlic cloves, cruched

5 personnes

- ▼ Wash, cut off the ends, string and chop the beans into medium size pieces.
- ▼ Fry the onions in oil in a big skillet until light brown
- ▼ Stir in the beans and sauté for around 10 minutes.
- ▼ Add the seasoning and lemon juice to the beans.
- ▼ Stir in the water and allow to simmer for 20 minutes or until tender.
- ▼ Serve cold.

Swisschard with Fava Beans

Silq bil Foul

5 garlic cloves
1 cup chopped green coriander
1/4 cup olive or vegetable oil
3 onions, chopped into thin slices
1/2 teaspoon salt
2 tablespoons oil for browning the garlic
1 cup small, dried fava beans, cooked
5 cups chopped swisschard, cleaned and washed

3 persons

▼ Prepare and cook as directed in swiss chard with blackeyed beans.

Mana'eesh with Cheese

Mana'eesh b'jibn

1 recipe mana'eesh dough
1 lb (1/2 kg) white salted cheese
1/4 cup butter, cut into thin slices
1 tablespoon sesame seeds

Topping for 3 mana'eesh

- Cut the white cheese into thin slices, and soak in water for 10 minutes.
- Drain well and mix with the butter slices and sesame seeds.
- Divide and sprinkle the cheese mixture among three bread rounds.
- Bake in a hot oven for 10 minutes.

Mana'eesh with Kishk

Mana'eesh b'kishk

1 recipe mana'eesh dough
3/4 cup kishk
1/2 cup olive oil
2 ripe tomatoes, finely chopped
1 onion, finely chopped
salt to taste
sesame seeds to taste
1/2 teaspoon hot chilli

Topping for 9 manaeesh

- Place the chopped tomatoes, onion and oil in a bowl and combine well.
- Stir in the salt, kishk and hot chilli pepper.
- Mix all ingredients well. Add some oil if the mixture is too thick. It should be easy to spread on the top of the dough.
- Divide among the rolled circles of dough.
- Bake in a hot oven 400°F for 10 minutes.

Mana'eesh Dough

Mana'eesh b'za'atar

2 cups flour
1/2 cup warm water
1/4 teaspoon salt
a dash sugar
2 teaspoons active dry yeast
1/3 cup oil

TOPPING
6 tablespoons seasoned, dried thyme
1/2 cup olive oil

5 persons

- Dissolve yeast in 4 tablespoons warm water until smooth.
- Sift sugar, salt and flour into a large bowl pour yeast liquid, oil and remaining warm water into center.
- Mix well then knead with your hands for a few minutes.
- Knead well on a flat surface then place in a well-oiled bowl and cover with a piece of cloth. Leave in a warm place to rise until double in size.
- Sprinkle a little flour onto a board, turn out the dough and knead for a minute.
- Divide into 5 balls and roll each ball into a 25 cm circle. Flute the edges of each circle with your fingertips. Sprinkle each circle with 2 tablespoons thyme mixture.
- Place on a lightly oiled baking sheet and bake in a hot oven for 4-5 minutes.

Okra in Oil

Bamia b'Zeit

- 2 lb (1 kg) fresh okra (tender)
- 4 medium-sized onions
- 2 whole garlic bulbs
- 1 tablespoon salt
- 3 lb (1 1/2 kg) ripe tomatoes, peeled and diced
- 1 cup olive oil
- 3/4 cup chopped fresh coriander
- 1/2 cup lemon juice
- 1 tablespoon ground, dried coriander

7 persons

▼ Cut off the stems of the okra then wash and drain.

▼ Sauté the okra, a few at a time, in oil until almost golden, then drain.

▼ Peel the onions and slice finely, then fry them with one whole peeled garlic bulb in the same oil that the okra was fried in.

▼ When the onions and garlic are lightly browned, add the okra, diced tomatoes, salt and lemon juice.

▼ Crush the remaining garlic cloves with the dried coriander, then add with the green coriander to the above ingredients.

▼ Pour half a cup of water over the okra and allow to boil over slow heat for half an hour without stirring.

▼ Garnish with slices of green pepper then serve cold.

Spicy Raw Kibbeh

frakeh

1 lb (1/2 kg) lamb or veal
100 g lard
1 onion
1 teaspoon each ground cumin, marjoram, basil, cinnamon and hot pepper
1 cup fine burghul
salt to taste
2 mint sprigs

6 persons

- ▼ Cut the lamb into medium-size pieces and flatten with a mallet until soft, removing any fat or gristle at the same time.
- ▼ Add the lard and salt to the lamb and beat again with the mallet until truly soft.
- ▼ Knead the lamb with two tablespoons burghul and set aside-covered with a plastic wrap.
- ▼ Crush the onion with the mint leaves.
- ▼ Add the seasoning, salt, and burghul to the mixture in the pestle and crush to soften.
- ▼ Add the lamb to the above mixture, knead and shape into a ball and set aside.
- ▼ Divide the mixture into egg size portions and press each in your palm so that it takes the shape of a fist.
- ▼ Place the fist shapes in a platter and sprinkle with a little hot pepper and garnish with pine nuts.

Swisschard with Blackeyed Beans

Silq bi lubia

1 cup blackeyed beans, cooked
5 garlic cloves
1 cup chopped green coriander
1/2 cup olive oil
3 onions, chopped into thin slices
1/2 teaspoon salt
5 cups chopped swisschard, cleaned and washed

3 persons

- Crush the garlic cloves and sauté in hot oil with the green coriander for 2 minutes.
- Stir in the chopped swisschard and leave for 2 minutes over medium heat.
- Add the cooked beans to the swisschard. Season and stir well.
- Cook over medium heat for 5 more minutes.
- Fry the onion slices in a little oil until brown in color.
- Serve the swisschard mixture garnished with the fried onions and a little lemon juice.

Shawarma

2 lb (1 kg) lamb fillet
100 g fat
1/4 cup each vinegar and olive oil
1 teaspoon each ground nutmeg, cardamom, cinnamon, cumin, cloves, allspice, black pepper,mistika, and salt

4 persons

- Cut the lamb fillet into thin strips (1/2 cm).
- Cut the fat into thin strips too.
- Mix the seasoming together with the vinegar and the olive oil.
- Combine the lamb and fat strips in a bowl with the seasoning mixture and let marinate overnight.
- Heat a large skillet very well. Add the lamb and fat strips and cook over high heat until the fat melts and the lamb strips turn brown.
- Serve with Tahinah sauce and salad.

Eggplants and Tomatoes in Oil
Maghmour

2 lb (1 kg) eggplants
5 small onions, peeled and chopped
2 lb (1 kg) ripe tomatoes, peeled
15 garlic cloves, peeled
2 tablespoon lemon juice
1/2 tablespoon salt
2 cups olive oil for frying
1/2 teaspoon dried mint leaves and a dash of pepper

3 persons

- ▼ Pare and cut the eggplants into medium-sized pieces.
- ▼ Sauté the eggplants in oil until tender, then add the chopped onions and stir fry until translucent.
- ▼ When the onions are almost golden in color, add the garlic and stir for 2 minutes.
- ▼ Add the peeled, chopped tomatoes to the eggplants, then add the seasoning and lemon juice.
- ▼ Crush 3 cloves of garlic with the dried mint, then add to the former ingredients and cook over medium heat.
- ▼ When the eggplants start boiling, reduce the heat and leave for 20 minutes, or until tender.

Lamb Spinal Marrow

Sanasel

250 g lamb spinal marrow
1/2 teaspoon salt
Juice of one lemon
2 tablespoons olive oil

3 persons

- Rinse the lamb spinal marrow and place it in a bowl with water to cover. Add salt.
- Cook over medium heat for 10 minutes.
- Drain the spinal marrow and let cool.
- Cut into 2 cm pieces, place in a serving dish and pour a mixture of the lemon juice and oil on the marrow pieces.
- Serve cold.

Tahinah Dip

Hommos bi tahinah

2 cups chickpeas (garbanzo beans)
1/2 teaspoon bicarbonate of soda
1 teaspoon salt
6 garlic cloves
3/4 cup lemon juice
1/2 cup tahinah paste
1/2 cup finely chopped parsley

5 persons

- ▼ Soak the chickpeas overnight in cold water with the bicarbonate of soda.
- ▼ Remove any beans that are floating and any stones that you might find.
- ▼ Cover the beans in clean water and bring to the boil over high heat until foam forms at the surface of the water.
- ▼ Remove the foam from the surface and let the chickpeas simmer for an hour and a half or until tender.
- ▼ Drain the chickpeas and purée in a blender or food processor.

- ▼ Crush the garlic with the salt, then beat in the tahinah and lemon juice.
- ▼ Stir in the chickpea purée and mix very well.
- ▼ Pour in small plates and garnish with a pinch of cumin, chopped parsley and olive oil.

Parsley in Tahinah Sauce

Ba'adounis Bi tahinah

1/2 cup tahinah sauce
1/2 teaspoon salt
3/4 cup chopped parsley
1/2 cup fresh lemon juice
1/2 cup water
3 garlic cloves

5 persons

- ▼ Crush the garlic with the salt, then stir in the tahinah and the water.
- ▼ Wash the chopped parsley very well, then drain.
- ▼ Add the parsley and lemon juice to the tahinah mixture and mix all the ingredients well.

Tahinah Dip with Minced Meat

Hommos Bi tahinah ma'a Lahm mafroum

1 recipe tahinah dip
6 oz (200 g) minced meat
1/4 cup pine nuts
1/4 cup vegetable oil
a dash of salt
a dash of pepper
a dash of cinnamon

5 persons

- ▼ Sauté the pine nuts in the oil until light brown, then remove from the oil.
- ▼ Season the meat, then fry in the same oil for 5 minutes, stirring constantly.
- ▼ Place the tahinah dip in platters, then cover with a mixture of meat and pine nuts.
- ▼ Serve immediately.

Stuffed Green Peppers in Oil
Mihshi Fleifleh b'Zeit

5 persons

- ▼ Cook as you would stuffed eggplants in oil, but instead of eggplants use 2 lb (1 kg) of green peppers.
- ▼ Wash the peppers well then remove the stem and fibrous portions that hold the seeds, then stuff.

Minced Green Peppers with Tomatoes
Shakshouka

3 green peppers
1 lb (1/2 kg) ripe tomatoes
3 tablespoons dried ground coriander
1/2 teaspoon salt
10 garlic cloves
a small amount of olive or vegetable oil

5 persons

- Wash and chop the peppers coarsely, then sauté in oil until tender.
- Peel and finely chop the tomatoes.
- Crush the garlic with the salt and dried coriander.
- When the peppers are tender, add the tomatoes and stir until tender.
- Add the garlic mixture to the tomatoes and peppers and stir well for 3 minutes .
- Remove from heat and serve cold.

Fried Kidneys

kalawi maklieh

6 lamb kidneys
1 onion, finley chopped
1 tablespoon vinegar
1/4 cup water
2 tablespoons lemon juice
1 tablespoon flour
3 tablespoons butter
a dash each salt, black pepper and allspice
1 tablespoon parsley, finely chopped

4 persons

- ▼ Skin and core the kidneys.
- ▼ Rinse briefly in cold water. Drain and dry with paper towels.
- ▼ Heat oil in a frying pan. Add chopped onion and stir until soft.
- ▼ Stir in Kidneys and fry for 5 minutes.
- ▼ Remove the kidneys from the pan and add the flour to the butter in the pan. Stir well, then add the remaining ingredients.
- ▼ Add the fried kidneys to the mixture and let simmer for 15 minutes.
- ▼ Serve hot, garnished with parsley.

SALADS

Beetroot Salad

Salatat Shamandar

1/2 cup vinegar
1/4 cup olive oil
1 lb (1/2 kg) cooked beets
2 onions cut into rings
1/2 cup chopped parsley
1 teaspoon salt

4 persons

▼ Place the onion rings in a salad bowl. Stir in the salt and vinegar.

▼ Peel then slice the beetroot and add the mixture in the bowl.

▼ Stir well and garnish with parsley.

Beetroot and Tahinah Salad
Salatat Shamandar bil Tahinah

2 lb (1 kg) beetroot
1/2 cup Tahinah paste
1/2 cup lemon juice
1 cup yoghurt
1 teaspoon salt
1 tablespoon finely chopped parsley
1 onion, finely chopped

10 persons

- Peel and dice the beetroot into small pieces.
- Wash and place in a saucepan.
- Cover with water and let simmer for 1/2 hour, covered.
- Marinate the chopped onions in lemon juice and salt.
- Beat the yoghurt and tahinah, add the lemon juice and onions and mix well.
- If mixture is thick, add 2 tablespoons water.
- Pour the tahinah mixture over the beetroot and stir well.

Swisschard Stalks in Yoghurt

Silq b'Laban

1 lb (1/2 kg) Swisschard stalks
2 cups yoghurt
5 garlic cloves
1/2 teaspoon salt

4 persons

▼ Wash, chop and drain the stalks, then boil as in (Swisschard stalks in tahinah sauce).

▼ Crush the garlic with the salt, then stir in the yoghurt.

▼ Add the swisschard stalks to the yoghurt, stir, then pour in small bowls and serve.

Carrot and Radish Salad
Salatat Jazar wa Fijil

- 4 medium carrots
- 4 large radishes
- 1 cup white or feta cheese, chopped
- 1/4 cup parsley, finely chopped
- 1/4 cup lemon juice
- 1 teaspoon salt
- 1/4 cup olive oil
- 2 garlic cloves
- 1/2 cup black olives for garnish

3 persons

▼ Wash, peel and grate the carrots and radishes.

▼ Crush the garlic and salt and beat in the lemon juice and oil.

▼ Pour the garlic lemon mixture over the grated carrots and radishes.

▼ Mix well then add the cheese pieces and garnish with the olives and parsley.

Cabbage Salad
Salatat Malfouf

- 1 small cabbage
- 2 garlic cloves
- 3/4 cup tahinah sauce or mayonnaise
- 1/4 cup each, vinegar, lemon juice and water

5 persons

▼ Remove the outer leaves and the core from the cabbage.

▼ Wash the leaves well then shred or chop very finely.

▼ Crush the garlic with the salt, then stir in the vinegar, lemon juice and water.

▼ Stir the above mixture into the tahinah and combine well.

▼ Add the shredded cabbage to the tahinah mixture. Stir well and serve.

Cucumber and Yoghurt Salad
Salatat Khiar ma'a Laban

- 1 lb (1/2 kg) cucumber
- 2 lb (1 kg) yoghurt
- 3 garlic cloves, crushed
- 1 tablespoon salt
- a dash of dried mint

10 persons

▼ Pare the cucumbers and slice them into thin circles.

▼ Crush the garlic with the salt and dried mint, then stir in the yoghurt.

▼ Add the cucumbers to the above yoghurt mixture and combine well.

Zucchini and Yoghurt Salad

Salatat Kousa b'Laban

1 lb (1/2 kg) zucchini
1/4 cup olive oil
1/4 cup parsley, finely chopped
1 tablespoon salt
3 cups yoghurt
4 garlic cloves

4 persons

- Wash and cut off the stems, then slice the zucchini into medium sized pieces.
- Cook in 2 cups of water and a dash of salt over medium heat for 20 minutes or until tender.
- Drain and set aside to cool.
- Chop the zucchini very finely.
- Crush the garlic with the salt and stir in the yoghurt.
- Add the chopped zucchini to the yoghurt mixture. Stir well.
- Pour into a platter then sprinkle with chopped parsley and olive oil.

Cucumber and Tomato Salad
Fattoush

1 lb (1/2 kg) cucumber
1 medium-sized lettuce
1/2 loaf arabic bread, toasted or dried
1 lb (1/2 kg) tomatoes
10 small radishes
1 tablespoon salt
5 garlic cloves
juice of 2 lemons
3 tablespoons vinegar
1/4 cup olive oil
1/2 cup fresh mint leaves
1 onion
1/2 cup each chopped parsley and purslane

5 persons

▼ Break the bread into small pieces.

▼ Chop the vegetables finely and combine them with the bread.

▼ Crush the garlic with salt and stir in the lemon juice, olive oil and vinegar.

▼ Add the garlic mixture to the vegetables and stir well.

▼ Sprinkle a little summac on the Fattoush and serve.

Pomegranate Salad
Salatat Ruman

- 3 cups finely shredded cabbage leaves
- seeds of one sour pomegranate
- juice of one lemon
- 1/4 cup vinegar
- 1/4 cup olive oil
- 1 garlic clove, crushed
- 1 teaspoon salt

4 persons

▼ Wash the shredded cabbage leaves well and drain.

▼ Peel and seed the pomegranate.

▼ Mix all the ingredients in a salad bowl and serve.

Kidney Bean Salad
Salatat al Fasoulia

- 1 cup dried kidney beans
- 1/2 cup pickles, finely chopped
- juice of half a lemon
- 1 onion, finely chopped
- 1 tablespoon vinegar
- 1/2 tablespoon salt
- 1/4 cup olive oil

4 persons

▼ Soak the beans overnight, then cook and drain.

▼ Add the pickles, onion, vinegar, lemon juice and salt to the beans and combine carefully.

▼ Pour the olive oil on the beans and garnish with green pepper rings.

Green Bean Salad
Salatat Lubyah Khadra

- 2 lb (1 kg) green (snap) beans (preferably tender)
- 1/2 cup lemon juice
- 1/4 cup olive oil
- 4 garlic cloves
- 1/2 tablepoon salt

5 persons

▼ Wash the beans, then string and snap off the ends.

▼ Drop into boiling water (to cover) add a pinch of salt and simmer covered until barely tender (15 minutes).

▼ Drain and put aside to cool.

▼ Crush the garlic with the salt, then add the lemon juice and stir the mixture well.

▼ Add the lemon mixture to the beans and combine well.

▼ Pour the olive oil on the beans and serve at once.

Lamb Tongue Salad
Lsanat Mtabbali

4 lamb tongues
2 tablespoons oil
2 onions, chopped
1 garlic clove, crushed
1/2 teaspoon each oregano, pepper, salt and ginger
Juice of one lemon

4 persons

- ▼ Wash tongue well and soak in cold water for 4 hours.
- ▼ Place the tongues in a pot with cold water and bring to the boil. Let boil for 15 minutes. Drain.
- ▼ Place the tongues again in a pot and cover with cold water and a teaspoon of vinegar, then let cook for one hour.
- ▼ Remove the tongues and reserve their water.
- ▼ When cold, take off the skin from the tongues and cut into slices.
- ▼ Sauté the onions and garlic in hot oil over medium heat. Then add 2 cups of the water that the tongues were cooked in. Stir.
- ▼ Place the tongue slices in an oven-proof dish, and pour the onion mixture, lemon juice and seasoning over the slices.
- ▼ Cover and bake in a hot oven for 30 minutes.

All Vegetable Salad
Salatat khodra

1 lb (1/2 kg) cucumber
1 lb (1/2 kg) tomatoes
1 head of lettuce
3/4 cup purslane leaves (optional)
1/2 cup mint leaves
4 spring onions
6 small round radishes
5 garlic cloves, crushed
1/4 cup olive oil and juice of one lemon
1/2 tablespoon each, vinegar and salt

7 persons

- ▼ Pare the cucumbers; peel the onions and pick out the leaves of the mint and purslane.
- ▼ Chop all the vegetables into medium-sized pieces.
- ▼ Season the vegetables with a mixture of garlic, lemon juice, vinegar and oil.

Potato Salad
Salatat Batata

6 potatoes, cooked
2 onions cut into rings
1/2 cup chopped parsley
1 tablespoon salt
a dash of pepper
juice of one lemon
1/2 cup vinegar
1 tablespoon mustard
1/2 cup olive oil

5 persons

- ▼ Peel and cut the potatoes into medium sized cubes.
- ▼ Place the onion rings in a bowl and stir in the vinegar, juice of one lemon, salt, oil and mustard.
- ▼ Add the potato cubes and stir well. Allow to marinate for 5 minutes.
- ▼ Place in a large salad bowl, garnish with the chopped parsley.

Parsley Salad
Tabbouleh

1 cup burghul (cracked wheat)
3 3/4 cups finely chopped parsley
1 lb (1/2 kg) tomatoes
3/4 cup finely chopped mint leaves
2 large onions
1/2 cup olive oil
1 tablespoon salt
juice of 4 lemons
a dash of black pepper

10 persons

- ▼ Remove any stones you might find in the cracked wheat, then wash and drain it well by squeezing it with your hands.
- ▼ Add the lemon juice to the cracked wheat and set aside.
- ▼ Wash the chopped parsley and mint, then drain well by squeezing out excess water.
- ▼ Chop the tomatoes very finely and add them to the cracked wheat.
- ▼ Chop the onions very finely and rub them with the salt and black pepper.
- ▼ Combine all ingredients with the cracked wheat and stir in olive oil.
- ▼ Garnish with lettuce leaves or cabbage leaves and serve immediately.

Tahinah Salad

Salatat Khodra bil Tahinah

1 cup chopped parsley
1 small onion, chopped
3 tomatoes
3 cucumbers
1/4 cup vinegar
1/2 cup tahinah
Juice of one lemon
1 teaspoon salt

4 persons

- Peel the cucumber and dice.
- Chop the tomatoes finely.
- Place the vegetables in a salad bowl.
- Mix the tahinah, vinegar, lemon juice and salt.
- If mixture is too thick, add a little water to it.
- Add the tahinah mixture to the vegetables and mix well.
- This salad is usually served with eggplants and rice.

Green Thyme Salad (1)
Salatat Za'atar Akhdar (1)

1 cup tender, green thyme leaves (thin variety)
1/4 teaspoon salt
1/4 cup olive oil
1 onion finely chopped
juice of half a lemon

3 persons

- Wash the leaves well and drain.
- Add the onion, lemon juice salt and oil to the leaves.
- Mix well and serve immediately.

Green Thyme Salad (2)
Salatat Za'atar Akhdar (2)

1 cup tender green thyme leaves (broad variety)
1 onion
1/4 teaspoon salt
1/4 cup olive oil
juice of half a lemon

3 persons

- Wash the leaves well and squeeze out excess water.
- Chop the onion very finely and rub with salt .
- Add the lemon juice to the above mixture and stir in the leaves.
- Pour the oil over the leaves and serve.

BEVERAGES

Apricot
Kamar Eddine

3 sheets apricot paste
6 cups hot water
1/2 cup sugar
1/4 cup orange blossom water

5 persons

▼ Cut the apricot paste sheets into small pieces then wash well.

▼ Place in a glass pot and let stand in hot water overnight.

▼ Put the mixture in the blender and blend then strain.

▼ Add the sugar and orange blossom water and stir well.

▼ Place in the refrigerator and serve cold.

Tamarind
Sharab Tamer Hindi

1 cup tamarind paste

7 persons

▼ Place the paste in a pot with 2 cups of water. Heat and bring to the boil.

▼ Remove from the heat and set aside.

▼ When cool squeeze the paste with your hands then place in a gauze sac with its juice and tie well. Add 6 cups of water. After an hour squeeze the sac well and remove.

▼ Stir in 3/4 cup of sugar or to taste.

▼ Serve cold.

Karkadeh

Charab al Karkadi

1 cup Karkadeh leaves
4 cups water
1 cup sugar

4 persons

- ▼ Wash Karkadeh leaves well, then place in a pot with 4 cups of water over medium heat.
- ▼ Let boil for 5 minutes then let soak overnight.
- ▼ Strain the Karkadeh leaves and pour the juice in a glass pitcher. Add sugar.
- ▼ Stir well until all sugar dissolves.
- ▼ Let cool in the fridge and serve chilled.

Liquorice Drink
Sharab Assous

1 cup liquorice powder
1/2 teaspoon bicarbonate of soda
10 cups of water

7 persons

- Place the liquorice powder with the bicarbonate of soda in a pot and add two glasses of water. Mix well.
- Pour the mixture in a gauze sac and tie well. Place the sac in a jar and add the required amount of water.
- Place in a refrigerator and let stand for 6 hours.
- Squeeze the sac well and strain.
- Serve cold.

Salep
Sahlab

1 teaspoon salep dissolved in a 1/4 cup milk
2 cups cold milk
Sugar according to taste

2 persons

- In a pot, pour the milk and the salep and milk mixture and bring to the boil, stirring, over gentle heat.
- When the mixture comes to the boil, remove from the heat and place in small cups. Garnish with a sprinkling of cinnamon.
- Serve hot.

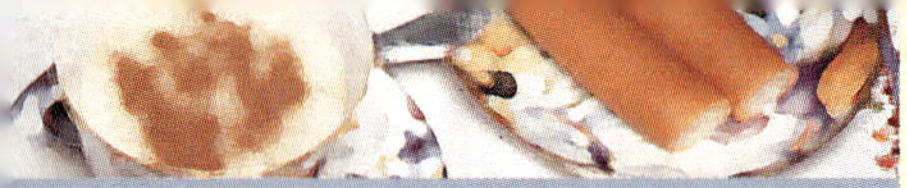

Turkish Coffee

Kahwa

2 teaspoons ground pulverized coffee
2 teaspoons sugar or to taste
4 coffee cups water

2 persons

- Put the sugar and water in a pot.
- Heat, add the ground coffee, and stir.
- Bring to the boil, stir, and bring to the boil again then pour into the coffee cups and serve.

Yoghurt Drink

Ayran

1/4 cup of yoghurt
3/4 cup of iced water
a dash of salt

1 person

- Fill a glass with the required amount yoghurt.
- Beat in the iced water. Add a little salt and serve immediatly.

Cinnamon Tea
Chaii al Kirfi

2 cups water
4 teaspoons powdered cinnamon
6 teaspoons sugar or to taste
1 cup chopped walnuts

3 persons

- Place the water with the powdered cinnamon in a pot and bring to the boil. Let simmer for 15 minutes over low heat.
- Stir in the sugar and leave for 2 more minutes.
- Remove from the heat and pour into tea cups.
- Garnish the cinnamon tea with 2 tbsp of chopped walnuts.
- Serve hot.

Green Tea
Shaii al Akhdar

4 cups water
1 tablespoon chinese green tea
3 tablespoons sugar
handful of fresh mint leaves

4 persons

- Place the tea leaves and mint in a warm tea pot.
- Pour the boiling water over the leaves add the sugar and mix well.
- Serve immediately.

SOUPS

Wheat Soup
Shourbat Kamh

1 lb (1/2 kg) meat with bones
1 cup wheat
4 tomatoes, peeled and chopped
2 tablespoons vegetable oil
16 cups water
1 onion, chopped
1/2 tablespoon cumin
10 peppercorns
1 cinnamon bark, broken into pieces
1/2 tablespoon dried ground coriander
1 tablespoon salt or to taste

6 persons

- ▼ Pick over the wheat and wash well. Soak in water overnight.
- ▼ Place all the spices in a bouquet garni or a piece of gauze tied to form a sac.
- ▼ Strain the wheat and place in a pot with the meat over low heat. Bring to the boil and add the bouquet garni.
- ▼ Reduce the heat and let cook for 40 minutes.
- ▼ Remove the meat and bouquet garni.
- ▼ Put the broth in a blender and blend.
- ▼ Add the meat, tomato, oil and salt to the wheat soup and let cook gently for 20 minutes.
- ▼ Serve hot.

Cracked Wheat Soup
Shourbat Burghul

1 cup cracked wheat (burghul)
5 onions, finely chopped
1 lb (1/2 kg) meat with bones
10 cups water
1/2 teaspoon powdered cardamom
1 tablespoon flour
a dash of pepper and salt to taste

6 persons

- ▼ Pick over then wash the burghul well.
- ▼ Pressure cook the meat and bones in the water for 30 minutes.
- ▼ Remove the bones from the broth. Then add the burghul and chopped onions to the meat.
- ▼ Pressure cook for 1 hour over low heat.
- ▼ Dissolve the flour in 1/4 cup of water then add with the powdered cardamon to the soup.
- ▼ Let boil for 2 minutes.

Green Wheat Soup

Shourbat Freekeh

10 cups water
1 lb (1/2 kg) meat with bones
1 cup freekeh (green unhulled wheat)
1 tablespoon flour
3 onions finely chopped
1 teaspoon each salt
and powdered cardamom
2 tablespoons chopped parsley

8 persons

- Pick over, wash and drain the freekeh.
- Place the meat and bones in a pressure cooker with 10 cups of water.
- Add the powdered cardamon,cover the pressure cooker and place over medium heat until the whistle starts turning.
- Reduce the heat and let cook for 1 hour.
- Remove the bones and meat from the soup with a large spoon. Set aside.
- Dissolve the flour in half a cup of water and add to the soup, stirring constantly.
- Add the salt and let cook for 4 minutes.
- Add the meat pieces to the soup and serve hot.

Bouillabaisse

Fish Soup

2 lb (1 kg) very fresh fish
4 whole shrimps in the shell
6 cups water
1/4 cup cider vinegar
1/2 cup olive oil
2 tablespoons minced celery leaves
4 medium-sized tomatoes, peeled and finely chopped
1 cup finely chopped leeks
1/2 cup chopped onions
1/2 cup chopped carrots
2 cloves garlic
a dash each, saffron, cardamon, turmeric, chilli
1 teaspoon salt
1 teaspoon black pepper
juice of one lemon
A few orange rinds
3 tablespoons chopped parsley

6 persons

- ▼ Clean the fish, scrub the shrimp and leave it in the shell.
- ▼ Heat the oil in a large pot and sauté all the vegetables for 5 minutes.
- ▼ Add the fish and shrimp to the above vegetables.
- ▼ Add the water, vinegar, seasoning and orange rind and bring to the boil.
- ▼ Cover the pot and leave over medium heat for 20 minutes.
- ▼ Remove the fish and shrimps from the pot and let the vegetables cook for 20 more minutes.
- ▼ Remove the shrimp from the shells and set aside.
- ▼ Remove the bones from the fish and place in a serving bowl with the shrimp.
- ▼ Strain the vegetables and blend in the electric blender until smooth.
- ▼ Return the blended vegetables to the fish stock in the pot and place over low heat.
- ▼ Brown 2 tablespoons flour in one tablespoon butter, then dissolve in half a cup of water.
- ▼ Add the flour mixture to the soup and stir over low heat for 3 minutes.
- ▼ Serve hot garnished with chopped parsley and the fish and shrimp pieces.

Rice Soup
Shourbat Riz

6 cups meat stock
3/4 cup ground or finely minced meat
1/2 teaspoon salt
a dash pepper
3 tablespoons parsley, finely chopped
1/2 cup short grain rice
1/2 teaspoon ground cardamon

6 persons

- ▼ Combine the meat with the salt, pepper and 2 tablespoons of chopped parsley.
- ▼ Knead the mixture then divide it into little balls and brown in a little oil. Drain.
- ▼ Bring the stock to the boil.
- ▼ Add rice to the stock and reduce the heat. Cook over low or gentle heat for 40 minutes.
- ▼ Just before serving, add the ground cardamom and remaining parsley. Stir to combine. Add the meat balls.
- ▼ Serve hot.

Pumpkin Soup
Shourbat Yakteen

- 1 lb (1/2 kg) pumpkin
- 1 lb (1/2 kg) potatoes
- 3 onions, chopped
- 3 tablespoons butter
- 9 cups chicken or meat stock
- 1 teaspoon each cinnamon and grated ginger
- 2 tablespoons chopped parsley
- 1 cup chopped tomatoes

8 persons

▼ Peel and dice the potatoes and pumpkin.

▼ Sauté in butter over medium heat until soft.

▼ Add the tomatoes, seasoning and stock, and bring to the boil.

▼ Reduce the heat and let cook for 15 minutes.

▼ Strain the soup and mash the vegetables in a vegetable grinder.

▼ Add the mashed vegetables to the soup and cook for 3 minutes.

▼ The soup should be a little thick. If too thick add a little water.

▼ Garnish with parsley and serve hot.

Spinach Soup
Shourbat Sabanekh

1/2 lb (1/4 kg) spinach
6 cups meat broth
6 oz (200 g) minced beef
2 tablespoons flour
1 tablespoon parsley, finely chopped
1 teaspoon ground cardamom
1 teaspoon salt
1/2 cup butter or ghee (for frying beef)
1/2 teaspoon salt
a dash of pepper
a dash of cinnamon

6 persons

- ▼ Remove the yellow leaves from the spinach, then wash, drain and chop very finely.
- ▼ Combine the beef, parsley and seasoning well.
- ▼ Divide the above mixture into small balls.
- ▼ Brown the meatballs in the butter or ghee.
- ▼ Remove the meatballs from the ghee, then brown the flour in the same ghee.
- ▼ Place the meat broth in a saucepan, add the flour and seasoning.
- ▼ Put the saucepan over medium heat, stir and bring to the boil.
- ▼ Reduce the heat and let simmer for 5 minutes.
- ▼ Meanwhile, put the chopped spinach in a saucepan with one cup of water.
- ▼ Place the saucepan over medium heat. Let boil for 3 minutes then drain the spinach.
- ▼ Add the chopped spinach and meat balls to the soup.
- ▼ Let the soup simmer for 5 more minutes, then serve.

Winter Vegetable Soup
Shourbat Khodra

3 cups diced leeks
2 cups diced turnips
1 cup diced carrots
1 cup finely shredded cabbage
2 tablespoons butter
1/2 teaspoon each cinnamon and pepper

6 persons

- Melt butter over low heat, then add the vegetables and sauté for 5 minutes.
- Add the seasoning and cover with hot water or meat stock.
- Cook for 20 minutes over low heat.
- Serve hot.

Chicken Soup
Shourbat Djaj

1 small chicken
8 cups cold water
1 onion
1 tablespoon salt
1 tablespoon butter
1 tablespoon parsley, finely chopped
a dash of pepper
1/2 cup vermicelli (thread-like noodles)

5 persons

- Clean the chicken and cut it into pieces, then place it in a saucepan with eight cups of cold water.
- Add the peeled onion to the chicken, cover the saucepan and let simmer over medium heat for 2 hours.
- Brown the vermicelli in the butter until golden then remove immediately.
- Strain the chicken broth, then add the vermicelli and let simmer over medium heat for 15 minutes.
- Add small chicken pieces to the strained broth; garnish with chopped parsley and serve.

Yoghurt Soup
Shourbat Laban

1 lb (1/2 kg) stewing meat, cubed
2 cups yoghurt
1 cup rice
2 tablespoons flour
2 teaspoons dried mint
2 tablespoons butter
1 teaspoon paprika

4 persons

- Wash the meat and place in a saucepan with 6 cups of water. Cook over low heat for 1 hour.
- Add the rice to the meat 20 minutes before the meat is completely cooked.
- Mix the yoghurt with the flour and dried mint.
- Add to the meat and rice mixture. Season and stir occasionally.
- Meanwhile, melt the butter, stir in the paprika and sauté a little over low heat.
- Add to the soup and serve immediately.

Lentil Soup

Shourbat Adas

1 cup brown lentils
1/4 cup rice, washed
6 cups water
1/2 teaspoon salt
1 onion, finely chopped
1/4 cup olive oil or ghee
1/2 cup parsley, finely chopped
a few cubes of toasted french bread
1/2 teaspoon powdered cumin
a dash of pepper

4 persons

- ▼ Remove any stones from the lentils, then wash well and drain.
- ▼ Place in a saucepan with the water and washed rice over medium heat and bring to the boil.
- ▼ Reduce the heat and simmer for half an hour.
- ▼ Remove from the fire and strain the lentils or purée through a vegetable strainer.
- ▼ While straining the lentils add half a cup of water into the vegetable strainer.
- ▼ Place the puréed lentils over medium heat and stir in cumin, salt and pepper.
- ▼ Brown the chopped onion in the oil or ghee, then add to the pureed lentils.
- ▼ Cook the lentils and the onion over medium heat for 5 minutes only.
- ▼ Sprinkle the soup with chopped parsley and bread cubes.

Chicken Soup with Semolina

Shourbat djaj bismeed

6 cups chicken stock
1/2 cup very fine semolina
1 teaspoon ground cardamom
1 teaspoon salt
2 tablespoons parsley, finely chopped
1 cup cooked chicken, cut into small pieces
1 onion, finely chopped

4 persons

▼ Place the stock over medium heat.

▼ Add the chopped onion and bring to the boil. Let boil for 5 minutes.

▼ Dissolve the semolina in half a cup of water. Add to the stock, stirring occasionally.

▼ Add the chicken pieces, cardamom and salt to the stock and simmer for 10 minutes.

▼ Garnish with the chopped parsley.

Tomato Soup
Shourbat Banadoura

4 cups tomato juice
1/4 cup short grain rice
2 tablespoons butter or ghee
3 garlic cloves
1 teaspoon dried coriander
1 teaspoon salt

3 persons

- Wash the rice then place it in a saucepan with the tomato juice.
- Bring to the boil, then reduce the heat and let simmer for 30 minutes.
- Crush the garlic with the dried coriander, then sauté in the butter or ghee until almost golden.
- Add the garlic mixture to the soup and let simmer for five minutes.
- Serve hot.

RICE & SPAGHETTI

Biryani Rice

Riz Biryani

2 chicken, cut into pieces
5 cups basmati rice
1 cup oil
5 onions, sliced
2 1/2 cups yoghurt
1 potato, blanched
1 egg
1 teaspoon cornflour
1 teaspoon each black pepper, cumin, dried coriander, cardamom, saffron and cinnamon (all ground)
1 tablespoon salt or to taste
1 tablespoon chopped garlic
10 cups water
3 mistica gum pieces
1/4 cup each fried almonds and pine nuts

10 persons

- ▼ Wash the chicken pieces and rub with salt. Wash again.
- ▼ Place the chicken pieces in a pot with the mistica, water and salt and cook for 40 minutes or until tender.
- ▼ Remove the chicken pieces and set aside.
- ▼ Beat the egg and cornflour, then beat in the yoghurt.
- ▼ Add the spices and 1/2 tbsp salt to the yoghurt and set aside.
- ▼ Sauté the onions in the oil until golden then remove from the oil.
- ▼ Place the onions over the chicken pieces in a big pot, then place the potato slices on top of the chicken.
- ▼ Pour the yoghurt over the potatoes and set aside.
- ▼ Pour 8 glasses of the chicken stock in a pot.
- ▼ Wash the rice and add to the stock with the oil the onions were fried in.
- ▼ Set aside until the rice absorbs all the liquid.
- ▼ Place the rice over the yoghurt mixture, cover with aluminum foil, and place the pot in a pan 1/4 filled with water.
- ▼ Bake in the oven for 30 minutes.
- ▼ Invert onto a serving dish and garnish with the fried nuts.

Bokhari Rice

Riz Boukhari

2 lb (1 kg) meat with bones
8 onions, chopped
4 cups basmati rice
1 cup oil
juice of 4 tomatoes
1 teaspoon each black pepper, cumin, cardamon (all ground)
1 tablespoon salt
4 carrots sliced thinly
6 cups hot water
1/4 cup each fried almonds and pine nuts

5 persons

- Mix the tomato juice with the spices and salt and set aside.
- Heat the oil to the point of fragrance then drop the meat and bones all at once and cover for 2 minutes. Uncover and stir well.
- Sauté the onions with the meat until almost golden brown.
- Add the tomato juice mixture and water and cook for 40 minutes or until the meat is tender.
- Remove the meat from the tomato sauce and put aside.
- Wash the carrots and boil in 2 cups of water.
- Add 1/2 tsp of salt and one tbsp of oil and cook for 5 minutes or until tender.
- Strain the cooking water of the carrots over the tomato mixture and put the carrots aside.
- Wash the rice and add to the tomato mixture.
- Place a soup spoon in the middle of the rice pot. If it remains standing then the quantity of the broth is just right. If not, there is too much broth.
- When the rice comes to the boil, reduce the heat and cook for 40 minutes.
- Invert on a serving plate and arrange the meat pieces and the carrots.
- Garnish with the almonds and pine nuts.

Fried Carrots with Rice

Ma'aloubet el Jazar

▼ Cook as you would fried eggplants with rice, but substitute 2 lb (1kg) carrots, peeled and sliced lengthwise for the eggplants.

Curried Rice

Riz bil Kari

4 cups rice
7 cups water
1 teaspoon salt or to taste
3 pieces mistica
2 stock cubes (maggi or knorr) for the rice
2 lb (1 kg) mutton, cubed
1 tablespoon curry powder
1 teaspoon ground garlic
1/2 cup vegetable oil
1/4 cup almonds, blanched slivered and fried
1/4 cup fried pine nuts
4 onions chopped
2 1/2 cups water for the meat
a dash of each cumin, dried coriander
a dash of pepper and cardamon (all ground)

8 persons

- ▼ Wash the rice, strain and place it in a pot with 7 cups of hot water.
- ▼ Stir in the 2 cubes of stock, add the salt and cook over low heat until done (20 minutes).
- ▼ Sauté the onions and meat in the oil, then add all the spices, curry and garlic.
- ▼ Boil the water and add to the above.
- ▼ Cook over low heat until meat is tender and the stock is reduced.
- ▼ Add the rice to the meat.
- ▼ Sauté the mistica in 1/4 cup oil, until it dissolves. Pour over the rice.
- ▼ Cover the pot and place it in a pan 1/4 filled with water.
- ▼ Bake in the oven for half an hour.
- ▼ Invert the rice and meat over a serving dish, garnish with the almonds and nuts. Serve.

Rice with Chicken

Kabsah el dajaj

2 chicken cut into 4 pieces
4 cups basmati rice
4 tomatoes finely chopped
4 onions finely chopped
1 tablespoon tomato paste
3/4 cup butter
1 teaspoon each black pepper, cumin and cardamom
1 1/2 teaspoons salt or to taste
7 cups hot water

8 persons

- ▼ Wash the chicken well. Rub with salt and wash again.
- ▼ Heat the butter and sauté the onions for 2 minutes.
- ▼ Add the chicken pieces and sauté for 5 minutes.
- ▼ Stir in the hot water, tomatoes and tomato paste.
- ▼ Season with the salt and spices and cook for 30 minutes.
- ▼ Wash the rice and place on top of the chicken and cook, covered for 40 more minutes.
- ▼ Invert on a plate and serve.

Cooked Rice (1)

Riz Matboukh

2 1/2 cups water
3/4 teaspoon salt
2 tablespoons butter
1 cup long grain rice (American)

5 persons

- Wash the rice in several waters then drain.
- Boil the required amount of water, then drop the rice gradually into the water.
- Add the salt and butter to the rice and stir slowly.
- Cook covered over low heat for 20 to 30 minutes.
- If the rice becomes too dry add 1/2 cup boiling water.
- Uncover the pot for the last 5 minutes of cooking and separate the grains by shaking the pot or fluffing the rice with a fork.

Cooked Rice (2)

Riz Matboukh

1 1/2 cups water
3/4 teaspoon salt
2 tablespoons butter
1 cup short grain rice

- Cook, as you would, long grain rice.

Rice With Chicken and Yoghurt

Riz b'Djaj wa Laban

3 chicken
4 cups rice
1/2 cup butter
1 1/2 cups yoghurt
8 cups water
10 cardamom seeds
3 pieces mistica
250 g minced meat, browned
2 tablespoons salt
1/4 cup pine nuts, fried
1/4 cup parsley, chopped

8 persons

- Cut the chicken into pieces and wash.
- Boil the chicken pieces in 8 cups of water.
- Add the cardamom seeds, mastica, salt and 3/4 cup butter. Cook for 40 minutes.
- Bone, skin, and cut the chicken into small pieces.
- Strain the chicken broth and drop the washed rice into it. Cook over low heat for 25 minutes.
- Sauté the chicken pieces in 1/4 cup butter for 2 minutes.
- Place the rice in a serving dish, then pour the yoghurt all over the rice.
- Arrange the chicken pieces and browned meat on top of the rice.
- Garnish with pine nuts and parsley.

Cooked Rice with Vermicelli

Riz bi Chaeriyyah

2 tablespoons ghee or butter
2 1/2 cups water
3/4 teaspoon salt
1 cup long grain rice
1/2 cup broken vermicelli or egg noodles

- Sauté the vermicelli in the butter until light brown in color, stirring constantly to avoid sticking and burning.
- Add the boiling water and rice to the vermicelli and cook as you would long grain rice.

Rice Cooked in Tomato Juice
Riz bil Banadoura

1 cup long grain rice
1/2 cup ghee or vegetable oil
1 small onion, finely minced
2 lb (1 kg) soft tomatoes
1 teaspoon salt
1/2 teaspoon paprika
1/2 teaspoon cinnamon
a dash of black pepper

5 persons

- ▾ Wash and squeeze the tomatoes by putting them through a vegetable strainer.
- ▾ Sauté the onions in the ghee until light brown in color.
- ▾ Add the strained tomato juice and the seasoning to the sautéed onions, stir and let come to the boil.
- ▾ Meanwhile, wash and drain the rice, then add to the above mixture and combine well.
- ▾ When the rice mixture boils, let simmer over low heat for another 25 minutes.
- ▾ Cover the rice mixture and put it aside to cool down, then invert over a platter without removing the pot.
- ▾ After five minutes, remove the pot carefully without destroying the shape of the mould.
- ▾ Serve hot.

Rice with Raisins and Almonds

Riz bi Zabeeb

2 cups short grain rice
1 onion finely chopped
200 g minced meat
1/2 cup raisins
3 cups chicken or meat stock
1/2 teaspoon each ground cardamom, saffron,
1/2 teaspoon each ground allspice, cinnamon
1/2 cup oil
1/2 cup almonds blanched, peeled, slivered
1 teaspoon salt

4 persons

▼ Wash the rice well and soak in warm water.
▼ Sauté the almonds in oil until golden.
▼ Remove the almonds from the oil and add the chopped onion to the oil.
▼ Sauté until tender.
▼ Add the minced meat to the onion and sauté for 5 minutes. Stir in the spices and raisin.
▼ Add the chicken stock to the meat mixture and bring to the boil.
▼ Strain the rice and add to the meat mixture.
▼ Let simmer for 5 minutes then stir gently with a fork.
▼ Cook, covered, over low heat for 30 minutes.
▼ Invert onto a serving plate and garnish with almonds.

Shrimp and Rice in Tomato Sauce
Kabsat Al Kraïdis

2 lb (1 kg) cleaned, deveined shrimp
1/2 cup vegetable oil
2 cups tomatoes, chopped
1 tablespoon tomato paste
4 cups basmati rice
4 onions, chopped finely
1 teaspoon each ground cumin, ginger, cardamom, cinnamon, allspice, dried coriander and paprika
1 tablespoon salt, or to taste
7 cups water

8 persons

▼ Sauté the chopped onions in the oil until translucent. Stir in the shrimps and sauté for 3 minutes.

▼ Add the chopped tomatoes, tomato paste, seasoning and salt to the shrimp mixture and stir well over medium heat.

▼ Add 7 cups hot water to the shrimp mixture. Bring to the boil and add the washed drained rice. Bring to the boil.

▼ Reduce the heat, and cook- covered - for 15 minutes.

▼ Pre-heat oven to 350°F.

▼ Place the shrimp pot in a tray filled with 4 cups water in the upper level of a hot oven. Let cook for 20 minutes.

▼ Invert the pot onto a serving plate and serve hot.

Rice with Minced Meat and Nuts

Riz b'Lahm

1/2 lb (1/4 kg) minced meat
1/2 cup ghee or butter
2 cups rice
1/2 teaspoon salt
1 teaspoon powdered cardamom
1/2 teaspoon cinnamon
1/2 teaspoon paprika
1/2 teaspoon saffron
2 tablespoons pistachio nuts
1/2 cup peeled almonds
2 tablespoons pine nuts
3 cups water

6 persons

- Remove any stones or hard kernels you might find among the almonds, pine nuts and pistachios.
- Blanche the almonds in boiling water for 3 minutes or until the skin comes off easily.
- Wash and drain the peeled almonds then put aside.
- Sauté the pine nuts in the ghee or butter, then remove the pine nuts and add the almonds. Sauté the almonds, stirring constantly until light brown in color.
- Remove the almonds and place the pistachio in the ghee and sauté for one minute.
- Remove from the ghee and set aside.
- Add the minced meat to the ghee and sauté for five minutes, then add the salt and seasoning.
- Add the required amount of water to the meat and let simmer over low heat.
- Wash and drain the rice, then add to the meat and water mixture and let simmer over low heat for 30 minutes.
- Fluff the rice with a fork and serve on a platter after garnishing it with the pine nuts, pistachios and almonds.
- Serve with roast chicken and yoghurt.

Spaghetti with Chicken and white Sauce

Ma' akarona b'Halib Wa b' Djaj

1 chicken (1 lb) or 1/2 kg cooked
1 cup grated parmesan cheese
3 1/2 cups white sauce
1/4 lb (125 g) spaghetti, cooked

5 persons

- Prepare the white sauce first. Remove from the fire and stir in the cheese immediately. Set aside
- Remove the bones from the cooked chicken.
- Place 1/3 of the boiled spaghetti into a greased baking dish, then sprinkle a 1/3 of the amount of shredded chicken meat over the spaghetti and cover the meat with half the amount of white sauce.
- Repeat this procedure and finish by covering the ingredients with the remaining amount of the white sauce.
- Place the dish in a hot oven for 20 minutes.
- Serve hot.

Spaghetti with Tomato Sauce
Ma'akarona b' Salsat al Banadoura

(1/2 lb) 1/4 kg spaghetti, cooked
(1 lb) 1/2 kg minced beef
1 small onion, finely chopped
1/2 cup butter
1/4 cup pine nuts
1/4 cup tomato paste
1 teaspoon salt
a dash of pepper
a dash of cinnamon

6 persons

- ▼ Sauté the pine nuts in the butter until light brown in color, then remove the pine nuts and place the beef and onion in the pan.
- ▼ Sauté the meat and onion for 5 minutes.
- ▼ Dissolve the tomato paste in 1 1/2 cups of water and stir into the meat mixture and let cook for 10 minutes.
- ▼ Remove from the fire, and add the pine nuts and seasoning to the meat mixture and stir well.
- ▼ Place the boiled spaghetti in a baking dish and pour the meat sauce over it.
- ▼ Combine the ingredients well and place the dish in a hot oven for 25 minutes.

Spaghetti with Yoghurt and Garlic
Ma' akarona b' Laban wa Toum

1/2 lb (1/4 kg) spaghetti, cooked
1/4 cup olive oil
4 cloves garlic, slivered
3 cups yoghurt
1 tablespoon chopped parsley
a dash of pepper
a dash of salt

4 persons

- ▼ Sauté the garlic slivers in the oil until light brown in color.
- ▼ Stir in the yoghurt, parsley and seasoning.
- ▼ Pour over the boiled spaghetti and serve immediately.

Spaghetti with Meat and White Sauce

Ma' akarona bhaleeb wa Lahm

2 lb (1 kg) spaghetti, cooked
2 lb (1 kg) minced meat
1 small onion, finely chopped
1/2 cup butter
1/4 cup pine nuts
1 teaspoon salt
1/4 cup tomato paste
1 cup water
3 1/2 cups white sauce
2 eggs, lightly beaten
2 cups grated parmesan cheese
a dash of pepper, and cinnamon

8 persons

- Prepare the white sauce(*) first. Remove from the heat and stir in 1 cup parmesan cheese.
- Add the lightly beaten eggs and set aside.
- Sauté the pine nuts in the butter until light brown in colour.
- Remove the pine nuts and sauté the onion and the minced meat over medium heat for 15 minutes.
- Add the seasoning, water and tomato paste to the meat. Cover and simmer over gentle heat for 15 minutes.
- Place half of the cooked spaghetti in a greased ovenproof dish.
- Top with the minced meat and cover with the remaining spaghetti.
- Pour white sauce on top and spread to cover the spaghetti.
- Sprinkle the remaining cheese on top and cook in a moderate oven for 20 minutes until golden brown.
- Serve hot.

EGGS

Scrambled Eggs with Eggplants

Ijjet Bayd bil Badinjan

1 lb (1/2 kg) eggplants
8 eggs
a dash of paprika
a dash of black pepper
1 cup vegetable oil
salt to taste

5 persons

- Pare and chop the eggplant into small cubes.
- Sauté the eggplant cubes in oil until light brown. Drain.
- Beat the eggs with the seasoning. Pour over the eggplant cubes in the skillet and stir once only.
- Cover the skillet and simmer over low heat for 5 minutes.
- Serve hot.

Scrambled Eggs with Potatoes

Bayd bil Batata

1 lb (1/2 kg) potatoes
4 eggs
1 cup vegetable oil
a dash of paprika
a dash of black pepper
1 teaspoon salt

3 persons

▼ Prepare and cook as directed in the recipe (Scrambled Eggs with Eggplants) using potatoes instead of eggplants.

Baked Eggs in Spinach

Bayd bil Forn

2 lb (1 kg) spinach
6 eggs
1 small onion, finely chopped
1/4 cup vegetable oil
1/2 teaspoon salt
a dash of pepper

6 persons

- ▼ Pick over and cut the roots and tough stems from the spinach. Chop finely and wash it in several waters until it is free from sand and soil. Drain.
- ▼ Place the spinach in boiling water to cover. Simmer covered for about 2 minutes over low heat. Drain.
- ▼ Sauté the onion in the oil. Add the spinach and stir over medium heat for 5 minutes.
- ▼ Pour the spinach in an ovenproof dish (diameter 30 cms)
- ▼ Make 6 equally spaced hollows in the spinach and break one egg carefully into each one. Season with salt and pepper.
- ▼ Bake in a hot oven for about 10 minutes and serve hot.

Fried Eggs with Tomatoes

Bayd Maa'li ma'a Banadoura

1 lb (1/2 kg) tomatoes
4 eggs
2 tablespoons butter
a dash of black pepper
a dash of paprika
1 garlic clove
1/2 teaspoon salt

5 persons

- ▼ Peel, seed and chop the tomatoes coarsely.
- ▼ Sauté the tomatoes in the butter over low heat for 5 minutes.
- ▼ Crush the garlic clove with the salt and add to the tomatoes.
- ▼ Beat the eggs well and add the seasoning.
- ▼ Pour the eggs over the tomatoes, stir once, and leave the mixture over low heat for 3 minutes.
- ▼ Serve hot.

Baked Vegetable Omelette

Ijjeh bil Forn

1 cup finely chopped parsley
1/4 cup milk
1/4 cup flour
6 eggs
3 medium-sized onions, finely chopped
1 zucchini, finely chopped or grated
1 sweet green pepper, finely chopped
1/2 tablespoon salt
1/2 teaspoon paprika
1/4 teaspoon black pepper
1/2 teaspoon baking powder
1/2 teaspoon vinegar
1/2 cup ghee or butter
1/2 cup toasted bread crumbs

5 persons

▼ Mix the flour and baking powder well. Add to the diced vegetables. Season.

▼ In another plate, break the eggs, add the milk, melted butter, and vinegar and beat well.

▼ Add the egg mixture to the vegetables and stir well.

▼ Grease a flat round baking dish and sprinkle it with the bread crumbs.

▼ Pour the omelette mixture over the bread crumbs and bake in a hot oven for 20 minutes or until the top turns golden.

▼ Serve hot.

Fried Vegetable Omelettes

Akras Ijjeh Makliyyah

7 persons

- Use the same ingredients as in the baked vegetable omelette recipe. But omit the milk and use 2 cups of vegetable oil for frying instead of the ghee.
- Prepare the egg mixture. Stir in the vegetable and flour mixture.
- Heat the oil in a big skillet. When the oil is very hot, spoon serving spoonfuls of the mixture into the hot oil to make small omelettes.
- When the omelettes are golden on both sides, remove from the oil and drain on absorbent paper.
- Repeat this procedure until all the mixture is used.

POULTRY

Curried Chicken

Djaj bil Kari

2 lb (1kg) chicken
2 small onions, coarsely chopped
5 cups water
1/2 cup flour
1 cup vermicelli
3 tablespoons curry powder
1/2 cup grated parmesan or gruyère cheese
4 tablespoons butter
pepper, cinnamon, salt

6 persons

- ▼ Draw, singe and wash the chicken. Place in a big pot over medium heat. Add the water, onions, and seasoning.
- ▼ When the water boils, cover the pot. Simmer over low heat for 40 minutes.
- ▼ Remove the chicken from the pot and strain the stock. Put aside.
- ▼ Cook the vermicelli in boiling water. Drain and add two tablespoons of butter and set aside.
- ▼ Brown the flour in the remaining butter. Add three cups of the strained chicken stock and stir constantly to avoid flour forming lumps. Add salt to taste.
- ▼ Add the curry powder to the above mixture. Stir constantly until slightly thick.
- ▼ Bone, skin and cut the chicken into small pieces.
- ▼ Place half the amount of vermicelli in the bottom of an ovenproof dish. Cover it with a little amount of parmesan cheese.
- ▼ Arrange half the amount of chicken pieces on top of the parmesan and pour a little curry sauce over the ingredients.
- ▼ Repeat the procedure until all the ingredients are used.
- ▼ Bake in a hot oven for 20 minutes.

Stuffed Chicken
Djaj Mihshi

2 lb (1 kg) chicken
1/4 cup pine nuts
1/4 cup pistachio nuts
6 oz (200 g) minced beef
1/2 cup ghee or vegetable oil
1 tablespoon flour
1 teaspoon each salt and pepper,
1 teaspoon each cinnamon, saffron
1 teaspoon powdered cardamom
1 cup long grain rice
1 bay leaf

8 persons

- Sauté the pine nuts in the ghee over medium heat. Remove from the ghee and add the pistachio nuts. Sauté and remove from the ghee.
- Sauté the minced meat in the ghee or oil. Add a teaspoon of salt and half the amount of the seasoning.
- Sauté the meat for 5 minutes and add two cups of water.
- Wash the rice and add to the meat. Stir and let simmer over low heat for 25 minutes.
- Draw, singe and wash the chicken well. Drain.
- Rub each chicken inside out with the rest of the seasoning.
- Mix the cooked rice mixture with the pistachio and pine nuts. Stuff the chicken and sew the opening with a needle and thread.
- Place the chicken(s) in a big pot. Add the bay leaf and 3 cups of water.
- When the water boils, remove the scum, add a little salt, and let simmer, covered, over low heat for 40 minutes.
- When done, remove the chicken from the pot and place in a baking dish.
- Bake in a hot oven for 15 minutes or until light brown.
- Dissolve the flour in a little amount of water. Add to the stock and stir until slightly thickened.
- Serve the chicken(s) garnished with a few sprigs of parsley. Pour the gravy in a separate dish and serve with the chicken(s).

Chicken with Milk and Rice

Saliq

2 chicken cut into pieces
3 cups rice
1/2 cup powdered milk
3 pieces mistica (gum arabic) for the broth
2 pieces mistica (gum arabic) for the ghee
1 cup cream
10 cardamom pods
1 tablespoon salt
1/4 cup ghee
12 cups water

10 persons

- Wash the chicken pieces and rub them with salt and flour. Wash again.
- Place the chicken pieces with the water in the saucepan. Bring to the boil and remove the scum. Add the cardamom pods, mistica and salt .
- Cook for 1 hour over low heat.
- Remove the chicken pieces and put aside.
- Strain the broth and place in a saucepan with the rice and cook over low heat.
- Dissolve the milk in 2 cups of water. Then add the cream and mix well.
- When the rice is cooked, add the milk mixture and stir well.
- Heat the ghee until fragrant and stir in the mistica.
- When melted pour immediately over the rice mixture and cover for 5 minutes.
- Stir the rice mixture and place in serving dish. Garnish with the reserved chicken pieces and serve.

Chicken with Peas and Rice

Djaj b'Riz wa Bisellah

2 lb (1kg) chicken
2 cups rice
1/2 cup ghee
1 onion, peeled
2 cups peas
1 tablespoon salt
6 oz (200 g) minced lamb or beef
2 tablespoons pine nuts
2 tablespoons pistachio nuts
1/2 cup blanched almonds
1/2 teaspoon each pepper, cinnamon,
1/2 teaspoon each cardamom, saffron

10 persons

- Draw, singe, wash and disjoint the neck from the chicken.
- Cut the chicken into 4 pieces. Place in a pot with the onion and 5 cups of water. Season with all the spices.
- When the water boils, let simmer over low heat, covered, for 30 minutes.
- Remove the chicken pieces from the stock. Set aside. Strain the stock.
- Sauté the pine nuts in the ghee until golden. Remove and set aside. Sauté the pistachios in the ghee. Remove and set aside. Finally sauté the almonds until light brown. Remove.
- Sauté the minced meat in the ghee for 10 minutes.
- Wash and drain the rice. Mix with the peas and add to the minced meat.
- Bone, skin and cut each chicken into pieces. Arrange the pieces on the bottom of a saucepan.
- Cover the chicken pieces with the rice mixture. Add three cups of the hot chicken stock to the rice mixture, carefully, so as not to disturb the rice. Let simmer, covered, over low heat for half an hour.
- Invert the saucepan over a large dish and leave in place for 5 minutes.
- Remove the saucepan carefully so as not to disturb the arrangement.
- Garnish the dish with the browned nuts. Serve immediatly.

Chicken with Green Pepper

Djaj bil Filfil

2 lb (1 kg) chicken, boned and skinned
2 onions, sliced
2 green peppers, sliced thinly
juice of 2 tomatoes
1 teaspoon ground black pepper
1 teaspoon ground cumin
1/2 tablespoon salt or to taste
1/2 tablespoon chopped garlic
1/4 cup vegetable oil
1/4 cup butter

5 persons

- Wash the chicken and cut into medium sized pieces.
- Put the oil and butter in a skillet and sauté the chicken pieces for 5 minutes.
- Remove from the oil.
- Sauté the onions, peppers and garlic in the same oil for 5 minutes.
- Add the salt, spices, tomato juice and chicken pieces to the onions and cook over low heat until the sauce is much reduced and the chicken pieces are tender (30 minutes).
- Serve hot.

Chicken with Rice

Djaj b'Riz

3 lb (1 1/2 kg) chicken
1/4 cup ghee
1/2 cup finely chopped onions
2 garlic cloves, crushed
1 large tomato
3 cups hot water
1 cup rice, uncooked
1 tablespoon minced parsley
2 teaspoons salt
1/2 teaspoon paprika
1/4 teaspoon black pepper
1/4 teaspoon saffron
1 bay leaf

5 persons

- Draw, disjoint and wash the chicken, then pat dry. Cut into 4 pieces.
- Sauté the onions and crushed garlic in the ghee over medium heat until tender.
- Remove the onions and garlic from the skillet. Drop the large chicken pieces first in the oil. Sauté until golden.
- Add the smaller pieces and sauté as well.
- Wash and chop the tomato coarsely. Add with the onions and garlic to the chicken pieces. Add all the other ingredients, except the rice.
- When the mixture boils, add the rice and cook covered for 45-60 minutes or until chicken pieces become quite tender.

Chicken in Tomato Sauce

Djaj bil Banadurah

3 lb (1 1/2 kg) chicken
2 onions, coarsely chopped
1/2 cup oil or ghee
2 garlic cloves
2 cups peeled chopped tomatoes
1 cup water
juice of 1 lemon
1 tablespoon salt
1/2 teaspoon eash turmeric, hot chili, black pepper, cinnamon and cardamom

4 persons

- Draw, singe, wash and disjoint the neck from the chicken.
- Cut the chicken into 4 pieces.
- Brown in the oil. Remove and set aside.
- Sauté the onions and garlic in the remaining oil.
- Add the chopped tomatoes to the onions and stir well. Add salt and seasoning.
- Let simmer covered over low heat for 5 minutes.
- Add the chicken pieces to the sauce and simmer over low heat for 1 hour.
- Serve hot with rice or alone.

Spicy Chicken

Djaj Harr

3 lb (1 1/2 kg) chicken, skinned and cleaned
4 tablespoons yoghurt
1 tsp chilli powder
1 teaspoon salt
2 tablespoons lemon juice
3 cloves garlic
2 small dried red chillies
2 teaspoons cumin seeds
1 tablespoon coriander seeds
1 small piece of ginger
1/4 cup butter, melted

4 persons

- Mix the chilli powder, pepper, salt and lemon juice together. Slash the chicken all over and rub the mixture into the cuts. Set aside for 1 hour.
- Marinate the chicken in a paste of the following: yoghurt, garlic, ginger, chillies, coriander and cumin blended in a food processor or blender.
- Spread the mixture all over the chicken, cover and leave overnight in the refrigerator.
- Preheat the oven to 200 degrees centigrade (400o F).
- Place the chicken on a rack in a roasting pan and pour over half the butter.
- Cook for one hour, or until tender.
- Halfway through cooking baste with the remaining butter.

Chicken with Summac

Mousakhan

2 lb (1 kg) chicken(s)
1 1/2 cups olive oil
8 onions finely chopped
3/4 cup summac
3 loaves arabic bread
1 teaspoon black pepper
1 teaspoon cinnamon
salt

6 persons

- Draw, singe, cut in halves and wash each chicken. Drain.
- Rub chicken pieces inside out with the seasoning.
- Mix the summac, some salt and chopped onions well. Add the olive oil to the mixture.
- In a baking tray, pour some olive oil.
- Split the loaves of bread into two and place in the tray.
- Spoon some onion mixture into the centre of each loaf. Place half the chicken(*) on top of each mound of onion mixture.
- Place a mound of onion and summac on top of each chicken.
- Cover chickens with the remaining split bread.
- Pour the remaining oil and summac over the bread.
- Bake in a hot oven for 40 minutes.
- Sprinkle bread lightly with water when the bread begins to brown and cover with aluminium foil.
- Serve hot.
- You may also shred the chicken into small pieces, and place the pieces over the onion mixture, then roll the bread in the shape of a swissrool, then slice and serve.

Chicken Pie

Fatirat Djaj

(2 lb) 1 kg chicken
2 onions
1/2 cup flour
1 medium-size can chopped mushroom
1/2 cup ghee
1/2 cup grated parmesan
1 puff pastry packet (380 g)
1 egg yolk, beaten
1/2 teaspoon each cinnamon, salt

6 persons

- Clean, wash and cut the chicken into 4 pieces.
- Place the chicken in a pot with one onion, 4 cups of water, one tablespoon salt and one teaspoon cinnamon.
- Bring to the boil, then reduce the heat, cover and cook for 40 minutes.
- Remove the chicken and set aside.
- Bone, skin and cut the chicken into small pieces.
- Drain the chopped mushrooms.
- Chop the remaining onion and sauté in the ghee until translucent. Stir in the mushrooms and seasoning.
- Add the chicken pieces and let cook over low heat, stirring occasionally.
- Add the flour to the above mixture and stir well.
- Stir in 2 cups of the chicken broth and cook for 5 more minutes. Set aside to cool.
- Roll out the puff pastry into a square of 1/4 cm thickness.
- Grease the bottom of a round pan and sprinkle a little flour on it.
- Place the rolled out dough onto the baking pan and pour the chicken mixture in the middle of the dough.
- Pull each corner of the square to the center of the dough forming an envelope.
- Brush the dough with the beaten egg mixture and bake in a preheated oven for 15-20 minutes.
- Serve hot.

Yoghurt Chicken

Djaj bil Laban

1 cup yoghurt
1/2 cup butter
10 peppercorns
10 cardamom pods
1 cinnamon stick
1 small piece ginger, chopped
2 cloves garlic, finely chopped
1 teaspoon chilli powder
2 teaspoons paprika
3 lb (1 1/2 kg) chicken pieces, skinned
salt to taste

6 persons

- Melt the butter in a deep, lidded frying pan.
- Add the onions, peppercorns, cardamom and cinnamon and fry until the onions are golden.
- Add the ginger, garlic, chilli powder, paprika and salt to taste and fry for 2 minutes, stirring occasionally.
- Add the chicken pieces and fry until browned.
- Gradually add the yoghurt, stirring constantly.
- Cover and cook gently for about 30 minutes.

Chicken in Yoghurt

Fattet al Djaj

1 large chicken
1/2 cup each pine nuts, almonds
2 lb (1 kg) yoghurt
2 cloves garlic
2 tablespoons tahinah
1 tablespoon lemon juice
1 tablespoon vinegar
1/2 cup chopped walnuts
1 1/2 loaves of pita (arabic) bread
1 cup rice
250 g ground meat
1 tablespoon chopped parsley
1/2 teaspoon each cinnamon and pepper

8 persons

- Clean and boil the chicken in five cups of water for 40 minutes. Let cool then bone and cut the chicken into medium size pieces.
- Brown the pine nuts in half a cup of vegetable oil and set aside. Brown the almonds in the same oil then set aside.
- Brown meat in the oil for 10 minutes, season with the pepper and cinnamon then add to the washed rice.
- Cook the rice mixture in the strained chicken stock for 30 minutes. Reserve 1/2 a cup of chicken stock.
- Cut the bread into cubes and toast the bread pieces in the oven until golden.
- Mix the crushed garlic with the lemon juice, vinegar and tahinah and stir in the yoghurt.
- Add salt to taste.
- Place the bread in a deep serving dish.
  Then sprinkle with the reserved chicken stock.
- Add the rice-meat mixture.
  Top with the yoghurt and walnuts.
- Garnish with the chicken pieces, parsley, almonds and pine nuts.
- Serve immediatly.

FISH

Fish Balls
Kafta Samak

3 lb (1 1/2 kg) fish
2 onions, finely chopped
1/2 cup parsley, chopped
1 cup white breadcrumbs
1 tablespoon salt
1 egg
1 teaspoon vinegar
1/2 teaspoon each black pepper, cumin and ground coriander
2 cups oil for frying
1/2 cup breadcrumbs for coating

6 persons

- Scale, clean, skin and remove any bones from the fish.
- Chop the fish and combine with onion and parsley and put through the meat grinder twice.
- Add breadcrumbs, egg, vinegar and seasoning and knead well.
- With moistened palms, shape into balls and chill in the refrigerator for 30 minutes.
- Coat fish balls with fine breadcrumbs and fry in hot oil until golden brown.
- Drain, then serve hot with salad.

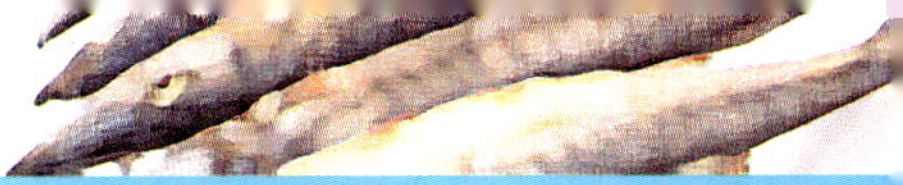

Prawns With Rice

Kraidis b'Riz

2 lb (1 kg) shelled, deveined prawns
1/4 cup butter
4 garlic cloves, peeled
1 onion, chopped
2 cups chopped peeled tomatoes
1/4 cup chopped parsley
1/4 cup chopped coriander leaves
2 1/2 cups water and 2 cups long grain rice
1/4 teaspoon each, turmeric, black pepper, cinnamon, paprika and chili pepper
1 teaspoon salt
2 cups water

4 persons

- ▼ Sauté the garlic in the butter and add the washed prawns to it.
- ▼ Remove the prawns when they turn pink.
- ▼ Sauté the chopped onion for 2 minutes, then add the chopped tomatoes and stir over low heat for 5 minutes.
- ▼ Add salt, seasoning, parsley, coriander and water, and let simmer for 10 minutes.
- ▼ Wash and drain the rice. Then add to the tomato mixture and bring to the boil. Stir well.
- ▼ Stir in the prawns and garlic. Cover the pot and let simmer over low heat for 20 minutes.
- ▼ Fluff the rice with a fork and serve on a platter after garnishing with lemon rinds.
- ▼ Serve hot with fresh salad.

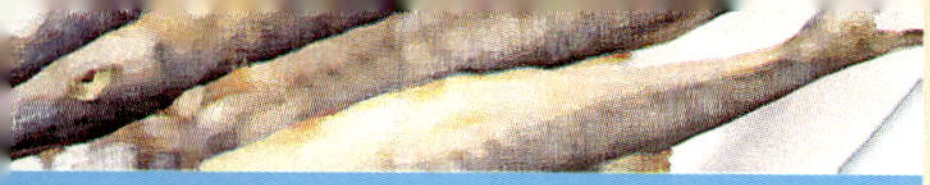

Baked Spicy Fish

Samkeh Harra

3 lb fish (1 1/2 kgs)
10 garlic cloves, crushed
2 tablespoons dried, ground coriander
1/2 cup walnuts, finely chopped
1 cup tahinah
1 cup lemon juice
3/4 cup olive oil
1/4 cup pine nuts
2 tablespoons vegetable oil to brown pine nuts
1 tablespoon salt
1/2 teaspoon each black pepper, paprika
1/2 teaspoon red hot pepper
2 cups water
1 small onion, chopped

4 persons

- Scale, remove the entrails and clean the fish.
- Rub it with one tablespoon salt and a little pepper, inside and outside.
- Rub the fish generously with olive oil. Place in a baking dish and bake in a hot oven for 25 minutes.
- Combine the tahinah with the lemon juice, salt and water.
- Brown the chopped onion and crushed garlic in a quarter cup of oil.
- Place the tahinah mixture over medium heat stirring constantly, for 5-10 minutes.
- When the oil floats on the surface of the tahinah mixture, stir in the browned onion, dried coriander and garlic and chopped walnuts and spices.
- Let boil over medium heat for another 2 minutes.
- Place the fish on a serving plate and pour the tahinah mixture on it.
- Brown the pine nuts in the remaining oil. Remove and garnish the fish with it.

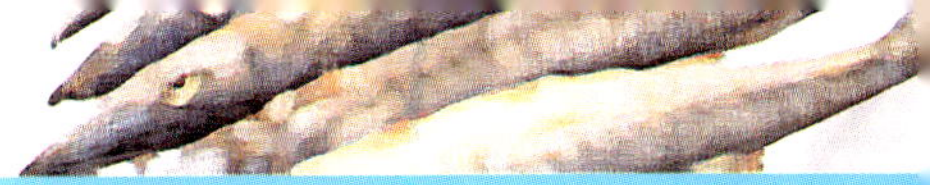

Fish Steak
Samak Qawarma

- 2 lb (1 kg) fish fillets or steaks
- 3 onions finely chopped
- 4 garlic cloves finely chopped
- 1 cup chopped, peeled tomatoes
- 1/2 cup water
- 1/4 cup lemon juice
- 1/4 cup oil or ghee
- 1/2 teaspoon each turmeric, hot chilli, pepper, cinnamon, ginger and saffron
- 2 teaspoons salt

5 persons

▼ Wash and clean the fish, then wipe dry and cut into steaks.

▼ Sauté the chopped onions and garlic in oil for 5 minutes.

▼ Add the chopped tomatoes, lemon juice and seasoning and simmer over low heat for 15 minutes.

▼ Place the fish steaks in the tomato sauce. Cover and simmer for 10 minutes.

▼ Serve hot with rice.

Spicy Fish with Coriander
Samkeh Harra bil Kozbara

- 2 lb (1 kg) fish or 2 lbs small fish
- 3 cups coriander, finely chopped
- 3 garlic bulbs
- 1/4 teaspoon red hot pepper
- 1 tablespoon salt
- 1 cup vegetable oil
- 1 teaspoon cumin
- 1/4 cup flour
- 1/2 cup lemon juice

4 persons

▼ Scale and clean the fish.

▼ Mix the flour, cumin and salt and dip the fish in this mixture until completely covered.

▼ Fry the fish in the hot oil until golden brown.

▼ Crush the garlic with one teaspoon of salt. Add to the chopped coriander.

▼ Sauté the above garlic mixture in the same oil the fish was fried in, until the garlic becomes tender.

▼ Add the hot pepper to the garlic mixture and let simmer for 5 minutes.

▼ Bone the fish and skin it. Flake it or cut it into small pieces.

▼ Remove the garlic mixture from the oil. Pour over the fish flakes and stir well.

▼ Place in a serving plate and serve cold with lemon juice.

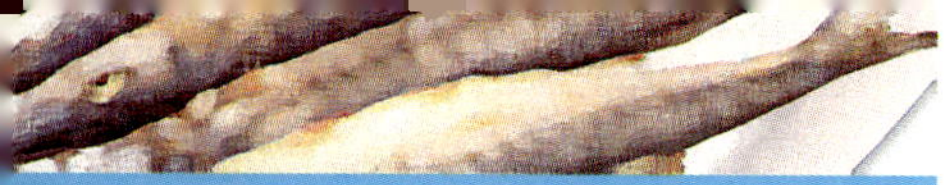

Fried Fish
Samak Makli

- 1/2 lb (1/4 kg) small fish
- 1/2 cup flour
- 1/2 teaspoon cumin
- 1 teaspoon salt
- 2 cups olive oil or vegetable oil

3 persons

▼ Scale (if necessary), clean, wash and drain the fish.

▼ Combine the flour, cumin and salt in a plate and dip each fish in the mixture until completely covered.

▼ Heat the oil very well. Fry the fish for 5 minutes or until golden brown.

▼ Garnish with lemon slices and serve hot.

Fish with Rice
Sayyadiah

2 lb (1 kg) fish
3 cups oil, for frying
7 onions, coarsely chopped
2 teaspoons salt
1/2 tablespoon cumin
1/2 cup seasoned flour (flour mixed with a little salt and cumin)
1 teaspoon black pepper
1 teaspoon saffron
2 cups long grain rice
2 3/4 cups water
1/2 cup pine nuts

SAUCE
4 onions thinly sliced
1/2 teaspoon salt
1/2 cup lemon juice
1/2 cup tahinah
1 cup water

- Skin, clean and cut the fish into medium-sized pieces.
- Dip the fish into the seasoned flour, then fry in hot oil until golden brown. Remove from the oil and allow to drain.
- Sauté the chopped onions in half a cup of the fish oil, until the onions are soft and tender. Remove from the oil and drain.
- Wash the rice in several waters. Drain.
- Bone the fish pieces and arrange them on the bottom of a sauce pan.
- Combine the rice and sautéed onions and pour over the fish pieces.
- Boil 4 cups of water with the salt, saffron and cumin. Remove from the heat.
- Place the fish and rice saucepan over low heat and add the boiling water without disturbing the rice. Shake the saucepan a little and let simmer on low heat for half an hour.
- Brown the pine nuts in half a cup of the fish oil. Remove and drain.
- Meanwhile, prepare the fish sauce. Place the onions, one cup of water and salt in a pot and let simmer over medium heat for 15 minutes. Set aside to cool.

- Add the lemon juice to the tahinah and combine well. Add the onion mixture to the tahinah and mix well until the sauce becomes smooth.
- Invert the fish saucepan over a big serving plate and leave for a few minutes.
- Remove the saucepan and garnish with pine nuts.
- Serve hot with tahinah sauce.

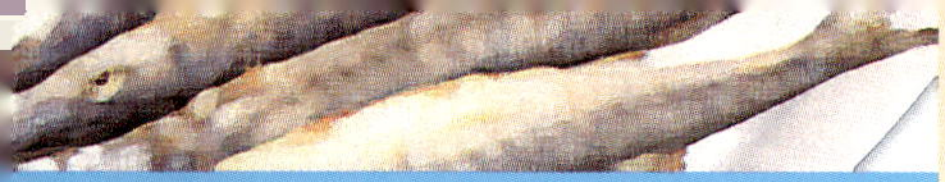

Baked Sardines

Sardine bil forn

2 lb (1 kg) White bait, cleaned
1 lb (1/2 kg) soft tomatoes
3 onions, cut into thin slices
1 tablespoon dried, ground coriander
5 garlic cloves
1/2 cup lemon juice
1 cup green coriander, chopped
a dash hot red pepper
1 tablespoon salt
1 tablespoon fresh ginger, grated
1/2 cup olive oil
1/2 teaspoon black pepper
a dash cumin

8 persons

- ▼ Rinse fish well in water. Drain.
- ▼ Place the onion slices in an oven-proof dish.
- ▼ Crush the garlic cloves with the salt and ground coriander. Add to onion slices.
- ▼ Wash, peel and chop the tomatoes finely. Add to the onion mixture.
- ▼ Stir in the grated ginger, lemon juice, green coriander, pepper, sardines and oil to the onion mixture. Combine well.
- ▼ Pre-heat oven to 400°F and bake the sardines for 15 minutes.
- ▼ Serve hot.

Baked Fish Steaks

Shara' eh Samak bil Forn

- 4 fish steaks
- 2 onions
- 5 garlic cloves
- 1/2 cup coriander, chopped
- 5 peeled sliced tomatoes
- 1/2 cup olive oil
- juice of one lemon
- 1 tablespoon salt
- 1/2 teaspoon black pepper
- 1/2 cup water

4 persons

▼ Chop the onions and garlic and sauté in olive oil for 5 minutes.

▼ Add the chopped coriander and sliced tomatoes to the onions and stir well.

▼ Add the seasoning, water and lemon juice and simmer over low heat for 15 minutes.

▼ Pour half the amount of sauce in an oven proof dish.

▼ Arrange the fish steaks on the sauce, then pour the remaning sauce on top.

▼ Bake in a hot oven for 20 minutes.

▼ Serve hot garnished with lemon slices.

Baked Fish with Tahinah

Samkeh bi Tahinah

- 4 lb (2 kg) fish
- 1 cup tahinah
- 10 onions thinly sliced
- 1 cup lemon juice
- 2 cups vegetable oil for frying
- 1 tablespoon vinegar
- 1 cup water
- 1 teaspoon salt
- 1 teaspoon cumin

6 persons

▼ Scale, clean and rub the fish (inside and outside) with a little salt and cumin.

▼ Brown the fish in the oil. Remove.

▼ Sauté the onions in the same oil until tender.

▼ Combine tahinah, lemon juice, vinegar, salt, cumin and water well. Stir in the onion slices.

▼ Make sure that the mixture is not too thick.

▼ Place the fish in a baking dish. Pour the Tahinah sauce over it and bake in a hot oven for 20 minutes.

▼ Serve hot.

Fish Stew

Yakhnet el Samak

3 filets of fish or 1 big fish
2 cups oil for frying the fish
1/2 cup pine nuts
1 tablespoon salt

SAUCE

1 lb (1/2 kg) onions
1 lb (1/2 kg) tahinah
1/2 cup oil for browning the onions
1 lb (1/2 kg) lemons
1 tablespoon pomegranate syrup (rib rumman)
2 lb (1 kg) each oranges, tangerines and bitter oranges
1 tablespoon vinegar
3 cups water

10 persons

- ▼ Clean, scale and cut the fish into big pieces.Sauté in oil.
- ▼ Remove the bones from the fish and set aside.
- ▼ Prepare the sauce as directed in kibbi in tahinah sauce.
- ▼ After the tahinah boils, drop the fish pieces in the sauce and let cook for 3 minutes.
- ▼ Serve garnished with pine nuts.
- ▼ Serve hot with rice.

VEGETABLES

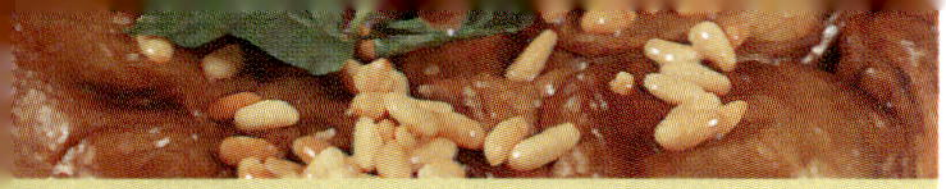

Stuffed Artichokes

Mihshi Ardi Shouki

10 artichokes
2 medium-sized onions
10 oz (300 g) minced meat
1/2 cup pine nuts
1/2 cup oil or ghee, to fry the meat
1/2 teaspoon salt
2 tablespoons oil to brown the flour
juice of one lemon
1 tablespoon flour
2 cups water
a dash of pepper

4 persons

- ▼ Clean, trim and discard the fuzzy centers from the artichokes.
- ▼ Place 2 cups of water in a saucepan and add a teaspoon salt and a tablespoon lemon juice.
- ▼ Arrange the artichokes in the pot with the lemon water and bring to the boil. Reduce the heat and simmer for 20 minutes.
- ▼ Remove the artichokes and reserve the water in which they were boiled.
- ▼ Arrange the artichokes in an ovenproof dish. Prepare the stuffing and fill the artichokes with it.
- ▼ Brown the flour in the oil and add the water the artichokes were boiled in .Stir well.
- ▼ Pour the flour mixture into the ovenproof dish and bake in a hot oven for 5 minutes.
- ▼ Serve hot with boiled rice.

Artichokes with Meat

Ardi Shouki b'Lahm

8 artichokes
2 onions, coarsely chopped
2 cups water
1 tablespoon flour
1 lb (1/2 kg) stewing meat, cubed
1/2 cup ghee or vegetable oil
1 teaspoon salt
juice of one lemon
a dash of pepper

5 persons

- ▼ Clean, trim and discard the fuzzy centers from the artichokes. Cut each into 4 pieces each. Wash.
- ▼ In a pot, place 2 cups of water, one teaspoon salt and one tablespoon lemon juice.
- ▼ Sauté the chopped onions and the meat cubes in the oil over medium heat for 15 minutes.
- ▼ Add the artichokes, water, salt, seasoning and lemon juice to the meat mixture. Simmer for 25 minutes.
- ▼ Lightly brown the flour over medium heat. Then add 1/4 cup of water, stirring constantly.
- ▼ Add the flour mixture to the artichokes and let simmer for 5 minutes.
- ▼ Serve hot with boiled rice.

Stuffed Pickled Eggplants
Makdous Al Badinjaan

6 lb (3 kg) small eggplants
1 cup garlic, crushed
2 cups walnuts
1/2 cup salt
1/2 teaspoon cayenne powder

5 persons

- Wash the eggplants and cut off the green stems.
- Place in a pan filled with water and press down with a small plate, so that all eggplants are immersed in water.
- Bring to the boil, then simmer over medium heat until the eggplants become soft, and yield when pressed with a finger.
- Remove the eggplants from the water and arrange- stems up- on a tray and set aside.
- Crush the walnuts. Then crush the garlic and salt and add to the walnuts. Season with the cayenne powder and mix well.
- Slit the eggplants lengthwise to form a pocket and fill with about a tablespoon of the above mixture.
- Pile the eggplants closely into glass jars then invert the jars over a plate and set aside for 2 days to drain.
- Turn the jars up right and pour olive oil on top of the eggplants to cover.
- Place a small piece of gauze on top of the oil and close the jars tightly.
- Set aside for 10 days.

Baked Stuffed Eggplants in Tomato Sauce

Sheikh al Mihshi

2 lb (1 kg) small eggplants
10 oz (300 g) minced meat
1/2 cup oil or ghee, to fry onions
1/4 cup pine nuts
2 cups vegetable oil, to fry the eggplants
1 medium-size onion, finely chopped
1/4 cup thick tomato paste
1 1/2 cups water, to dissolve the paste
1 tablespoon lemon juice
1 teaspoon salt
a dash pepper

4 persons

- Brown the pine nuts in oil. Remove and drain.
- Sauté in the remaining oil the minced meat and chopped onions. Season and let simmer for 15 minutes. Remove from the heat and add the pine nuts.
- Pare the eggplants leaving a few patches unpeeled. Sauté until light brown.
- Slit each eggplant lengthwise to form a pocket and fill with the stuffing.
- Arrange the eggplants in an ovenproof dish.
- Dissolve the tomato paste in the water and lemon juice and pour over the eggplants.
- Bake in a hot oven for 15 minutes.
- Serve hot with boiled rice.
- You may add a few slices of green pepper during baking, to give a nice flavour.

Stuffed Eggplants with Yoghurt
Fattet al Badinjan

1 lb (1/2 kg) small eggplants
1/2 cup pine nuts
1cup ghee or vegetable oil
1/4 cup ghee to fry the pine nuts
2 lb (1 kg) tomatoes, peeled and finely chopped
1/4 cup ghee to brown the bread
3 cups yoghurt
2 garlic cloves
10 oz (300 g) minced meat
2 cups toasted arabic bread cut into small pieces
1 teaspoon salt
a dash of pepper, paprika and cinnamon

4 persons

- Lightly brown the pine nuts in the ghee. Remove and drain.
- Sauté the minced meat in the remaining oil or ghee. Season and let simmer over low heat for 10 minutes.
- Wash the eggplants and scoop out the pulp leaving a shell 1/4 cm thick. Wash again.
- Mix the sautéed meat with half the amount of the pine nuts and fill the eggplants with this stuffing.
- Sauté the stuffed eggplants in the oil.
- Place the peeled, chopped tomatoes in a large ovenproof dish. Arrange the sautéed eggplants on top of the tomatoes.
- Add one teaspoon salt to the eggplants and allow to come to the boil. Reduce the heat and simmer for 30 minutes.
- Brown the bread in the oil and drain.
- Crush the garlic with a dash of salt and add to the yoghurt.
- When the eggplants are done, remove from the tomatoes and set aside.
- Place the browned bread pieces in a serving dish, and add 2 cups tomato sauce to it.
- Crush the garlic with half teaspoon salt and mix it with yoghurt.
- Pour the yoghurt mixture over the bread and tomato sauce. Arrange the eggplants over the yoghurt mixture.
- Garnish with the remaining browned pine nuts and their oil. Serve immediatetly.

Fried Baked Eggplants

Badinjan bil Forn

4 lb (2 kg) large round eggplants
2 cups vegetable oil, to fry the eggplants
3 lb (1 1/2 kg) very ripe tomatoes
1 teaspoon salt
3 garlic cloves

STUFFING
2 onions, finely chopped
13 oz (400 g) minced meat
1/4 cup ghee or butter
1/4 cup pine nuts

5 persons

- ▼ Pare and cut the eggplants lengthwise into 1/2 inch thick slices.
- ▼ Fry the slices in hot oil until brown. Drain on absorbent paper.
- ▼ Sauté the pine nuts until light brown. Remove and drain.
- ▼ Add the minced meat and onions to the remaining oil and sauté. Season and let simmer for 15 minutes.
- ▼ Remove the meat from the heat and add the browned pine nuts.
- ▼ Arrange a layer of the fried eggplant slices in an ovenproof dish. Cover with the stuffing then top with the remaining layer of eggplants.
- ▼ Peel and coarsely chop the tomatoes.
- ▼ Crush the garlic with the salt and add to the tomatoes.
- ▼ Cover the eggplants with the tomato and garlic mixture.
- ▼ Bake in a hot oven for 15 minutes.
- ▼ Serve hot with cooked rice.

Fried Eggplants

Badinjan Makli

one big, round eggplant
vegetable oil
salt

- ▼ Pare and cut the eggplant into 1/2 inch slices.
- ▼ Sprinkle a little salt on the slices and leave aside for 15 minutes. Wipe dry.
- ▼ Fry the slices in hot oil until golden brown.
- ▼ Remove from the oil and drain.
- ▼ Serve hot or cold with yoghurt.

Fried Baked Eggplants in White Sauce

Mousaka'a

2 lb (1 kg) big, round eggplants
3 cups white sauce
1/2 cup parmesan cheese
1/2 teaspoon salt
a dash of nutmeg, a dash of black pepper
2 eggs, lightly beaten

MEAT STUFFING
2 large onions finely chopped
2 cloves garlic, crushed
2 tablespoons oil for frying the meat
1 lb (1/2 kg) minced meat
2 cups tomatoes, chopped
1/4 cup tomato paste
1/4 cup lemon juice
1/4 cup parsley, chopped
3/4 cup water
a dash of black pepper, saffron and cinnamon
salt to taste

8 persons

- ▼ Pare and cut the eggplants lengthwise into 1/2 inch thick slices.
- ▼ Sprinkle the slices with salt and leave for 30 minutes.
- ▼ Dry the slices with a towel and fry them in hot oil until brown. Drain on absorbent paper.
- ▼ Fry onion and garlic in oil for 5 minutes. Add the meat and stir well for another 5 minutes.
- ▼ Add the tomatoes, tomato paste, lemon juice, parsley, water and seasoning to the meat. Cover and simmer for 15 minutes.
- ▼ Prepare the white sauce(*), remove from heat and add 1/4 cup parmesan cheese.
- ▼ Arrange a layer of the fried eggplant slices in an oven proof dish.
- ▼ Cover with the meat sauce and top the meat sauce with a remaining layer of eggplants.
- ▼ Add the beaten eggs to the white sauce and stir well.
- ▼ Spread the white sauce on top of eggplants and sprinkle the remaining cheese on top.
- ▼ Bake in a hot oven for 15 minutes.
- ▼ Serve hot with either cooked rice or cooked spaghetti.

Fried Eggplants with Rice

Ma'aloubet el Badinjan

3 lb (1 1/2 kg) large round eggplants
1 lb (1/2 kg) stewing meat, cubed
4 cups water
1 tablespoon salt
1/2 cup pine nuts
1 1/2 cups long grain rice
1/4 cup ghee or butter, to brown the pine nuts
1/2 teaspoon paprika
1/2 teaspoon cinnamon
1/2 teaspoon saffron
2 1/2 cups vegetable oil, to fry the eggplants

- ▼ Pare and cut the eggplants lengthwise into 1/2 inch thick slices.
- ▼ Fry the eggplant slices in hot oil until golden brown. Drain.
- ▼ Wash the meat cubes. Place in a pot and add the required amount of water.
- ▼ When the water boils, remove the scum and season.
- ▼ Cook, covered, over low heat for 40 minutes.
- ▼ Wash the rice in several waters. Drain.
- ▼ Remove the meat cubes from the pot. Strain the meat broth (stock).
- ▼ In a large saucepan, sprinkle 2 tablespoons uncooked rice and place the meat cubes over the rice.
- ▼ Arrange the eggplant slices over the meat cubes and along the sides of the saucepan.
- ▼ Add the remaining amount of the rice over the eggplant slices. Pour the hot meat broth onto the rice without disturbing the arrangement.
- ▼ Cook, covered over low heat for 40 minutes.
- ▼ Invert the saucepan over a large serving dish. Remove the saucepan carefully.
- ▼ Serve hot, garnished with pine nuts.

Eggplants Stew
Badinjan bil Lahm

2 lb (1 kg) eggplants
1 lb (1/2 kg) stewing beef
5 medium tomatoes, cubed
4 garlic cloves, crushed
1 cup green coriander
1 1/2 cups water
3 onions, coarsely chopped
1/2 teaspoon each dried coriander, pepper
1/2 cup vegetable oil

5 persons

- Peel and cut the eggplants into small cubes. Sprinkle the clubes with salt and let stand for 30 minutes. Wash and drain.
- Sauté the onions then the meat in the oil for 15 minutes.
- Add the tomatoes, garlic, salt, chopped coriander and spices to the meat mixture and stir over medium heat.
- Add the water to the above ingredients and bring to the boil.
- Remove the meat from the heat and add the browned pine nuts.
- Reduce the heat and let simmer over low heat for 30 minutes or until the meat is thoroughly cooked.

Lentils and Eggplants in Oil
Habbat Rumman

1 cup lentils (big, flat-seed variety)
1/2 cup vegetable oil
4 small eggplants, peeled and chopped
4 garlic cloves
2 cups onion rings
1/2 cup flour
1/2 cup pomegranate syrup
10 cups water
a dash of black pepper, salt to taste

3 persons

- Boil the lentils until soft.
- Add the eggplants and shake-don't stir-the pot.
- Let cook until the eggplants are tender.
- Crush the garlic cloves.
- Disslove the flour in one cup of water. Add the pomegranate syrup, salt and garlic. Mix well.
- Add the above mixture to the lentils, shake the pot and let boil until slightly thick in consistency.
- Fry the onion rings in oil until golden.
- Place the lentil mixture in a serving dish, and serve garnished with the onion rings.

Swisschard with Fava Beans
Silq bil Foul

1 cup small, dried fava beans, cooked
5 cups chopped swisschard, cleaned and washed
5 cloves garlic
1 cup chopped green coriander
1/4 cup olive or vegetable oil
3 onions, chopped into thin slices
1/2 teaspoon salt
2 tablespoons oil for browning the garlic

2 persons

▼ Prepare and cook as directed in swisschard with blackeyed beans.

Stuffed Carrots
Jazar Mehshi

2 lb (1 kg) big carrots
2 cups vegetable oil for frying the carrots
1/4 cup dried tamarind paste
1 tablespoon salt
3 1/2 cups water

STUFFING
3/4 cup rice
2 tablespoons ghee or oil
200 g minced beef
a dash each, allspice, cinnamon
1 teaspoon salt

4 persons

- Peel and wash the carrots then hollow out or core the centers leaving a shell 1 cm in thickness.
- Wash the rice in several waters. Drain.
- Add the seasoning, salt, minced meat and ghee to the rice. Stir to combine.
- Three-quarters fill each carrot with the stuffing, then place in a saucepan and sauté in oil. Arrange in a pot.
- Soak the tamarind in 2 cups water. Then strain or squeeze out the juice on top of the stuffed carrots.
- Add 3 1/2 cups water and cook-covered-until it comes to the boil.
- Reduce the heat and cook over gentle heat for 1 1/2 hours.
- Serve hot.

Fried Carrots with Rice

Ma'aloubet el Jazar

▼ Cook as you would fried eggplants with rice, but substitute 2 lb (1 kg) carrots, peeled and sliced lengthwise for the eggplants.

Walnut and Chilli Dip

Mohammara

2 cups ground walnuts
1/2 cup breadcrumbs
1/2 teaspoon tabasco (chilli sauce)
1/4 cup olive oil
a dash cumin,a dash salt
2 tablespoons lemon juice
1 tablespoon pomegranate syrop (rib rumman)
1/2 teaspoon sugar
1/4 cup water
1/2 cup ketchup
1/2 cup prepared, ground chilli (red hot pepper in oil)

8 persons

- ▼ Sprinkle the breadcrumbs with the water and set aside.
- ▼ Mix the walnuts with the red hot pepper and oil and let stand for 30 minutes.
- ▼ Add the damp bread crumbs to the walnut mixture. Stir in the ketchup, sugar, cumin, lemon juice and pomegranate syrup. Mix well .
- ▼ Season according to taste. If the mixture is too thick add a little more oil.

Fried Cauliflower with Rice

Ma'aloubet el Arnabeet

1 medium-sized head cauliflower
vegetable oil

5 persons

▼ Cook as you would Fried Eggplants with Rice but substitute 3 lb (1 1/2 kg) of cauliflower (cut into medium-sized pieces) for the eggplants.

Fried Cauliflower

Arnabeet ma'ali

1 medium-sized head cauliflower
vegetable oil

5 persons

▼ Cut off the tough end of the stem, remove the leaves and cut the cauliflower into small florets.

▼ Soak in cold salted water, then wash and drain the florets.

▼ Deep fry in hot oil until golden. Remove and drain.

▼ Serve hot or cold.

Cauliflower Stew
Yakhnet Arnabeet

- 2 lb (1kg) cauliflower
- 1 tablespoon flour
- 13 oz (400 g) stewing beef or lamb, cubed
- 5 garlic cloves
- 1 cup green coriander, chopped
- 1 cup vegetable oil
- 3 cups water
- 1/4 cup butter
- 1/4 cup lemon juice
- salt and pepper

4 persons

- ▼ Wash the meat and place in a saucepan with 3 cups of water. Bring to the boil, remove the scum, reduce the heat and simmer for 30 minutes.
- ▼ Meanwhile cut off the tough end of the stem, remove the leaves and cut the cauliflower into big florets. Wash and drain.
- ▼ Sauté the florets in hot oil until light brown.
- ▼ Remove from the oil and drain.
- ▼ Crush the garlic cloves and sauté with the chopped coriander in 1/4 cup butter.
- ▼ Add the sautéed coriander and garlic to the florets and meat. Add the lemon juice and cook over low heat, for one hour.
- ▼ Brown the flour over medium heat and dissolve in two tablespoons of water.
- ▼ Add the flour only 5 minutes before removing the cauliflower pot from the heat.
- ▼ Serve with cooked rice.

Mashed Pumpkin with Burghul
Kibbet Lakteen

3 cups cooked strained pumpkin
2 1/2 cups fine burghul
1/2 cup flour
1 cup finely chopped green coriander
1 teaspoon each ground cumin, marjoram, cinnamon, dried coriander, caraway and turmeric

STUFFING
1 cups cooked chickpeas
4 cups onions, chopped into small slices
1/2 teaspoon each cumin and dried coriander
salt to taste
1/4 cup sumac
3 tablespoons pomegranate syrup (rib rumman)
a dash of powdered chilli
1/2 cup olive oil

7 persons

▼ Peel and scrape away the seeds and fibers from the pumpkin then dice into medium size pieces.

▼ Place the pumpkin pieces in a pressure cooker with half a cup of water and let cook over low heat for 25 minutes. Drain and set aside .

▼ When cool, squeeze out excess water from the pumpkin pieces and add to the (dry) burghul. Stir well.

▼ Add the dried coriander, salt and seasoning to the burghul and knead well. Set aside.

▼ Sauté the onions over medium heat until translucent then add the stuffing seasoning and the chick peas. Stir well.

▼ Remove the stuffing from the heat and add the sumac and pomegranate syrup .

▼ Grease a rectangular ovenproof dish (14 x 28) with olive oil.

▼ Knead the pumpkin mixture and the flour well until smooth and divide into two equal parts.

▼ Pre-heat the oven to 400°F.

▼ Knead the first half between the palms of the hand and press down in the bottom of the dish until it forms one smooth layer (1 cm thick).

▼ Place the stuffing over this layer and then cover the stuffing with the second half of the burghul mixture.

▼ Smooth the surface with a little olive oil then cut into medium size pieces.

▼ Bake in a hot oven for 20 minutes.

▼ Serve cold.

Fried Pumpkin Slices
Yakteen Ma'ali

1 lb (1/2 kg) pumpkin
1 cup vegetable oil
Juice of one lemon
3 garlic cloves
1/2 teaspoon salt

4 persons

- ▼ Cut the pumpkin into slices, 1/2 centimeter thick, then peel.
- ▼ Fry the slices in hot oil over medium heat.
- ▼ Turn the slices and brown on the other side.
- ▼ Remove from the oil and drain on absorbent paper.
- ▼ Crush the garlic cloves with the salt and mix in the lemon juice.
- ▼ Arrange the pumpkin slices on a serving platter and pour the lemon juice mixture on top.

Colocasia (Taro) with Beef

OL'AS bilahem

3 lb (1 1/2 kg) colocasia
7 cups water
1 lb (1/2 kg) stewing beef
1 tablespoon salt
1/4 cup butter or ghee
5 garlic cloves
1/4 cup lemon juice
1/2 cup parsley, finely chopped
1/4 cup salt for soaking the colocasia
1/2 tablespoon dried, ground coriander

7 persons

▼ Peel the Colocasia tubers like you peel potatos, then slice evenly.

▼ Soak the slices in salt for 30 minutes. Rinse well to get rid of the slimy texture.

▼ Wash beef pieces in a pot with 7 cups of water. Bring to the boil, removing the scum as soon as it appears. Add salt.

▼ Cook the meat-covered-over gentle heat for 30 minutes.

▼ Add the colocasia slices and lemon juice to the meat in the pot and cook-covered-over gentle heat for 30 minutes or until done.

▼ Do not stir the colocasia, just shake the pot a little.

▼ Crush the garlic cloves with the dried coriander and brown over medium heat in the ghee.

▼ Add the garlic mixture with the melted ghee to the colocasia slices and let cook fo 5 minutes.

▼ Add the chopped parsley and serve hot with rice.

Stuffed Cucumber

Khiar Mahshi

2 lb (1 kg) cucumber, medium sized
2 cups vegetable oil for frying
1/3 cup dried tamarind paste
1 tablespoon salt
5 cups water

STUFFING
200 g minced beef
3/4 cup rice
a dash each allspice, cinnamon
1/2 teaspoon salt or to taste
2 tablespoons ghee or oil

5 persons

- Wash the cucumber and cut off the stems.
- Core or hollow out the centers leaving a shell 1/2 cm thick. Soak in water.
- Drain and set aside.
- Wash the rice well and drain.
- Add the minced beef, seasoning, salt and oil to the rice. Stir to combine.
- Soak the tamarind paste in 2 cups water.
- Stuff the cucumbers and brown in oil as in "stuffed carrots".
- Squeeze out the juice from the tamarind onto the stuffed cucumber. Add the water.
- Place the saucepan over medium heat and bring to the boil.
- Reduce the heat and cook-covered-for one hour.
- Serve hot.

Jew's Mallow with Chicken (1)

Melokhiyya masriyyah

1 lb (1/2 kg) Jew's mallow leaves
2 lb (1 kg) chicken
10 cups water
1 lb (1/2 kg) stewing meat with bones
1 tablespoon salt
1 1/2 cups coriander, chopped
1 tablespoon dried ground coriander
1/4 cup ghee or butter
3 garlic bulbs, peeled
1 onion
1/2 teaspoon each pepper, cinnamon
2 tablespoons lemon juice

7 persons

- ▼ Draw, singe, clean and cut the chicken into pieces.
- ▼ Place the chicken pieces in a pot with the stewing meat, bones and onion.
- ▼ Add 10 cups of water and bring to the boil. Remove the scum, reduce the heat and cook for one hour. Season.
- ▼ Wash the Jew's Mallow leaves and spread them on a big cloth to dry.
- ▼ When completely dry, chop finely using a special knife.
- ▼ Crush half the amount of garlic cloves with the dried coriander. Add the other half (uncrushed) to the meat and allow to cook in the pot.
- ▼ Sauté the crushed garlic with the dried and fresh coriander in the ghee or butter. Stir the ingredients until they become soft.
- ▼ When the meat and chicken are well done, remove them from the broth. Bone the chicken and strain the broth.
- ▼ Put the strained broth over medium heat in a pot with the stewing meat, the garlic and coriander, lemon juice and the Jew's mallow leaves. Salt to taste.
- ▼ Allow to come to the boil then reduce the heat and simmer for 5 minutes.
- ▼ Serve in a large serving platter garnished with the chicken pieces.
- ▼ This dish is eaten with cooked rice along with one minced onion mixed in a cup of vinegar.

Jew 's Mallow with Chicken (2)

Melokhiyya Warak

1lb (1/2 kg) Jew's mallow leaves
1lb (1/2 kg) chicken
1 onion for the broth
1 cup chopped coriander
13 oz (400 g) stewing meat with bones or chicken
3 garlic bulbs
1/4 cup dried ground coriander
1/2 teaspoon black pepper
1 tablespoon salt
1/2 cup ghee or butter, for frying the leaves
1/4 cup ghee or butter, for frying the coriander
7 cups water

6 persons

- ▼ Wash the Jew's mallow leaves in several waters. Spread on a piece of cloth to dry.
- ▼ Draw, singe, clean and cut the chicken into medium-sized pieces. Place in a pot with 7 cups of water, stewing meat and bones and one onion. Bring to the boil then remove the scum. Reduce the heat, add half the amount of garlic cloves to the meat, and cook for one hour.
- ▼ Sauté the Jew's mallow leaves in half a cup of ghee for 10 minutes over medium heat.
- ▼ When the meat is well done, remove from the broth and strain the broth. Bone the chicken.
- ▼ Add the stewing meat and 4 cups of strained broth to the Jew's mallow leaves. Bring to the boil and reduce the heat.
- ▼ Crush the garlic with the dried coriander.
- ▼ Heat the ghee or butter and sauté the crushed garlic, dried coriander and fresh coriander and black pepper for 5 minutes.
- ▼ Add the above mixture to the Jew's mallow leaves and cook over low heat for half an hour.
- ▼ Garnish the Jew's mallow with pieces of chicken anda serve with boiled rice.

Stuffed Squash with Tomates

Karaâ Mahchi bil Banadoura

4 lb (2 kg) squash
4 lb (2 kg) soft tomatoes
1/2 tablespoon salt
5 garlic cloves
2 tablespoons ghee

STUFFING

3 cups short grain rice
1 lb (1/2 kg) minced beef
4 tablespoons ghee or butter
1/2 tablespoon salt
1/2 teaspoon each allspice, cinnamon
a dash black pepper

8 persons

- Peel the squash and cut off the stem ends. Keep the stems aside.
- Core and scoop out the centers leaving a shell 1 cm thick. Soak in water for 3 minutes.
- Wash the squash from inside and outside. Drain.
- Wash the rice in several waters. Drain.
- Add the seasoning, minced meat, salt and ghee to the rice. Stir well to combine.
- Three-quarters fill the squash shells with the rice mixture.
- Sauté the washed stems in a little ghee in a saucepan.
- Arrange the stuffed squash on top of the stems in layers.
- Strain the tomatoes in a vegetable strainer. Add the tomato juice to the stuffed squash with the salt.
- Bring to the boil and let cook-covered- over gentle heat for 1 1/2 hours.
- Just before the squash is done, crush the garlic with the salt and add to the squash in the saucepan.
- Serve hot.

Stuffed Zucchini in Tomato Sauce
Kousa Mihshi bi Banadoura

4 lb (2 kg) meduim-sized zucchini
1 teaspoon salt for the sauce
3 cups short grain rice
1 lb (1/2 kg) minced meat
1/2 cup ghee or butter
4 lb (2 kg) ripe tomatoes or 1/2 cup tomato paste
1 teaspoon salt
1/2 teaspoon pepper
a dash of paprika and cinnamon
juice of 1/2 a lemon
4 garlic cloves

10 persons

- Wash the zucchini and cut off their stem ends.
- Scoop out the centers leaving a shell 1/2 cm thick. Keep the pulp to make "Zucchini pulp in oil".
- Wash the zucchini again and drain.
- Wash the rice in several waters and drain.
- Add the seasoning, ghee and minced meat to the rice. Mix well.
- Three-quarters fill the zucchini shell with the above mixture and shake each after filling so that the stuffing is well distributed.
- Peel and finely chop the tomatoes, and place in a saucepan with 2 tablespoons ghee and one teaspoon salt.
- Sauté the tomatoes over low heat for 5 minutes or until quite soft.
- Arrange the stuffed zucchini over the tomatoes in the saucepan and add one or two cups water to cover the zucchini.
- When the water comes to the boil, reduce the heat and cook for 1 hour.
- Just before the zucchini is done, crush the garlic and add with the lemon juice to the zucchini.
- Serve hot with the tomato sauce.

Stuffed Zucchini in Yoghurt

Kousa Mihshi b'Laban

3 lb (1 1/2 kg) yoghurt, cooked
4 lb (2 kg) medium-sized zucchini
4 garlic cloves
1 teaspoon salt
1 teaspoon dried mint leaves

STUFFING
1 lb (1/2 kg) minced meat
3 cups short grain rice
1/4 cup ghee or vegetable oil
1/2 teaspoon pepper
1/2 teaspoon cinnamon

10 persons

- Prepare and stuff as you would "Stuffed Zucchini with tomatoes".
- Place the stuffed zucchini in a pot with 4 cups water and half a teaspoon of salt.
- Bring to the boil, reduce the heat and cook for 40 minutes.
- Meanwhile, cook the yoghurt and add to the zucchini. Simmer over low heat for 15 minutes.
- Crush the garlic with the mint leaves and add to the yoghurt for the final 5 minutes of cooking.
- Serve hot.

Fried Stuffed Zucchini with Lemon

Ablama b'Hamod

▼ Cook as you would "Fried Stuffed Zucchini in Tomato sauce", but substitute 1/4 cup of lemon juice dissolved in one cup of water for the tomatoes.

Fried Stuffed Zucchini in Yoghurt

Ablama b'Laban

▼ Cook as you would "Fried Stuffed Zucchini in Tomato Sauce" but substitute 2 lb (1 kg) cooked yoghurt for the tomatoes.

▼ Add the cooked yoghurt to the zucchini only 10 minutes before serving.

▼ Serve hot with cooked rice.

Fried Stuffed Zucchini in Tomato Sauce

Kousa Ablama bi Banadoura

2 lb (1 kg) small zucchini
3 lb (1 1/2 kg) ripe tomatoes
(or 3 tablespoons tomato paste)
1 teaspoon salt
1 1/2 cups vegetable oil
2 garlic cloves
1/2 teaspoon dried mint
1 tablespoon flour

STUFFING

1 lb (1/2 kg) minced beef or lamb
2 onions, finely chopped
1/2 cup pine nuts
1/2 cup vegetable oil or butter
1/2 teaspoon each salt, pepper and cinnamon
a dash of black pepper

10 persons

▼ Brown the pine nuts in the butter. Drain well.

▼ Add the minced meat, chopped onions and seasoning and sauté in the remaining butter for 15 minutes.

▼ Remove this mixture from the butter and add the pine nuts and mix well.

▼ Wash and cut off the stem ends of the zucchini.

▼ Scoop out the centers leaving a shell 1/2 cm thick. Keep the pulp for use in another recipe.

▼ Wash the zucchini again. Drain.

▼ Fill each zucchini with the stuffing until really full.

▼ Lightly brown the stuffed zucchini in hot vegetable oil. Remove and arrange in a saucepan.

▼ Peel the tomatoes and strain in a vegetable strainer. Add the tomato juice to the zucchini and bring the sauce to the boil. Reduce the heat and cook over low heat for 15 minutes.

▼ Brown the flour in one tablespoon butter. Add a little tomato sauce to the flour and stir well until the flour dissolves completely. Pour the sauce back over the zucchini.

▼ Crush the garlic with the dried mint and add to the zucchini. Allow to boil for 3 minutes with the mint .

▼ Serve hot with cooked rice.

Zucchini Pulp in Oil

Lubb el Kousa b'Zeit

1 1/2 cups zucchini pulp
1 onion, finely chopped
4 garlic cloves
1/4 cup lemon juice or pomegranate syrup
1/4 cup olive oil
1/2 teaspoon dried mint leaves
1/2 teaspoon salt

5 persons

1st Method:

- Sauté the chopped onion in the oil until light brown. Add the zucchini pulp and salt and stir for 5 minutes.
- Crush the garlic with the dried mint and add the lemon juice. Pour this mixture over the pulp and stir for several minutes.
- Remove from the heat and serve cold.

2nd Method:

- Cook the zucchini pulp and the chopped onion until soft and tender.
- Remove from the heat, drain and add the crushed garlic, dried mint and lemon juice to the pulp.
- Mix well and pour olive oil on top of the mixture. Serve cold.

Stuffed Swisschard Leaves

Mihshi Silq

1 lb (1/2 kg) swisschard
1/2 teaspoon salt
1/4 cup butter or ghee

STUFFING
1 cup short grain rice
13 oz (400 g) minced beef or lamb
1/2 cup ghee or butter
1/2 teaspoon each salt, pepper, cinnamon

5 persons

- Pick over, remove the tough stems and wash the swisschard very well.
- Blanche by dropping the leaves in boiling water and leaving them for half a minute only.
- Remove promptly and cook as you would, stuffed grape or vine leaves.
- Serve hot with swisschard in tahinah sauce.

Zucchini Stew
Yakhnet Kousa

4 lb (2 kg) zucchini
1 lb (1/2 kg) stewing meat or lamb, cubed
1/4 cup vegetable oil
1 small onion, chopped
1 tablespoon salt
1 lb (1/2 kg) ripe tomatoes or 2 tablespoons tomato paste (dissolved in 1 cup water)
a dash of pepper and cinnamon

8 persons

▼ Place the meat, seasoning and onion in a pot with 1/4 cup of vegetable oil. Sauté over low heat for 20 minutes.

▼ Peel and chop the tomatoes and add to the meat.

▼ Wash the zucchini, cut off the stem ends and chop into medium-sized pieces. Add to the meat.

▼ Cook the ingredients over low heat for 25 minutes without stirring.

▼ Serve hot with cooked rice.

Zucchini Stew with Yoghurt
Yakhnet Kousa b'Laban

2 lbs (1 kg) zucchini
13 oz (400 g) stewing meat, cubed
1/2 cup ghee or butter
2 onions, coarsely chopped
1 teaspoon salt
1 lb (1/2 kg) yoghurt
3 garlic cloves
1/2 teaspoon each dried mint leaves, salt
a dash of pepper and cinnamon

5 persons

▼ Wash the zucchini and cut off the stem ends. Chop into meduim-sized pieces.

▼ Sauté the chopped onions in the butter for 5 minutes.

▼ Add the meat to the onions and sauté over low heat for an additional 5 minutes.

▼ Add one cup of water and season the meat. Cook over low heat for 20 minutes or until the meat is well done.

▼ Add the zucchini to the meat and cook for 15 minutes.

▼ Cook the yoghurt(*).

▼ Crush the garlic with the mint, and add to the cooked yoghurt.

▼ Add the cooked yoghurt to the zucchini and simmer for 5 minutes over low heat.

▼ Serve hot with cooked rice.

Green Bean Stew
Yakhnet Lubyah

- 2 lb (1 kg) fresh green beans
- 1 lb (1/2 kg) stewing beef, cubed
- 1/2 cup vegetable oil
- 1 1/2 cups boiling water
- 1 tablespoon each salt and flour
- 1/2 teaspoon pepper
- 1/2 teaspoon cinnamon

5 persons

▼ Wash the meat cubes and sauté in the vegetable oil with the seasoning for 15 minutes.

▼ String and snip off the ends of the green beans. Snip each bean into two and wash.

▼ Add the beans to the meat and sauté for 15 minutes.

▼ Add the boiling water to the meat and beans and cook over low heat for 3/4 hour.

▼ Just before removing the beans from the heat, brown the flour in one tablespoon of butter and dissolve it in 1/2 cup water, stirring constantly.

▼ Add the dissolved flour to the beans and allow to boil for 5 minutes.

▼ Serve hot with cooked rice.

Green Bean Stew in Tomato Sauce
Yakhnet Lubyah bil Banadoura

▼ Cook as you would "Green Bean Stew" but add 2 lbs (1 kg) tomatoes to the ingredients.

▼ Peel, seed and chop the tomatoes finely.

▼ Add the chopped tomatoes to the browned meat with the green beans. Cook as directed.

▼ Serve hot with cooked rice.

Stuffed Cabbage Leaves

Mihshi Malfouf

3 lb (1 1/2 kgs) head of cabbage
1/4 cup ghee
1 teaspoon salt
1 garlic bulb, peeled
1/2 cup lemon juice

STUFFING

1 1/2 cups short grain rice
1lb (1/2 kg) minced meat or lamb
1/2 cup vegetable oil
1 teaspoon salt
1/2 teaspoon each pepper, cinnamon

5 persons

- Remove the core from the cabbage and separate the leaves.
- Blanche the leaves – a few at a time – and remove from the water quickly. Drain.
- Flatten the central veins of the leaves, discarding them if they are too tough to roll.
- Cut the large leaves into halves and leave the small ones whole.
- Prepare the stuffing and stuff and roll as directed in "Stuffed grape vine leaves in oil".
- In a saucepan, place a layer of blanched unstuffed cabbage leaves, 1/4 cup of ghee and the garlic cloves.
- Arrange the stuffed leaves on top of the garlic cloves and cover with a plate turned upside-down to keep them in place.
- Cover the stuffed leaves with boiling water and place the saucepan over medium heat until the water comes to the boil.
- Reduce the heat add lemon juce, and cook until the water evaporates (one hour).
- Turn the stuffed leaves onto a platter and serve with yoghurt.

Stuffed Grape Vine Leaves
Mihshi Wara'a Enab

1 lb (1/2 kg) grape vine leaves
3 onions
1/4 cup ghee or butter
2 lb (1 kg) ripe tomatoes (optional)

STUFFING
13 oz (400 g) minced meat
1/2 cup ghee or vegetable oil
1 cup short grain rice
a dash each paprika, cinnamon
1 teaspoon salt

7 persons

- Cut off the stems and wash the grape leaves.
- Drop the leaves-a few at a time-in boiling water. Remove quickly.
- Wash the rice in several waters. Drain and add the seasoning. Mix well.
- Add the ghee and meat to the rice.
- Peel the onions and cut into rings. Place the rings in the bottom of a saucepan.
- Peel the tomatoes and cut into rings. Arrange 1/2 the rings on top of the onion rings in the saucepan. Add the salt and 1/4 cup ghee.
- Stuff and roll the blanched vine leaves as directed in "Stuffed Grape Vine Leaves in Oil ".
- Arrange the stuffed leaves in a saucepan over the onion and tomato rings.
- Cover the layer(s) of grape vine leaves with a plate turned upside-down, to keep them in place.
- Cover the layers of grape vine leaves with hot water so that the water is 2 cms above the level of the grape vine leaves, and bring to the boil. Reduce the heat and cook for 50 minutes or until most of the water evaporates.
- Turn the stuffed leaves onto a large platter and serve with yoghurt.

Okra Stew

Yakhnet Bamia

2 lb (1 kg) fresh green okra
1 tablespoon ketchup
1 cup coriander, minced
2 garlic bulbs, peeled
juice of one lemon
1 tablespoon salt
13 oz (400 g) stewing beef, cubed
2 lb (1 kg) tomatoes or (1/2 cup paste)
2 cups vegetable oil, for frying the okra
1/2 teaspoon each paprika, cinnamon
2 tablespoons ghee to brown the meat
1 onion coarsely chopped

5 persons

- ▼ Sauté the chopped onion and the meat in the ghee for 5 minutes.
- ▼ Peel and finely chop the tomatoes and add to the meat. Season and stir the mixture until the tomatoes become quite soft.
- ▼ Add half the amount of garlic to the meat and tomato mixture with 1 1/2 cups of water.
- ▼ Cook, covered for 25 minutes over low heat.
- ▼ Cut off the stems, wash and drain the okra.
- ▼ Lightly brown the okra in hot oil. Drain.
- ▼ Crush the remaining garlic cloves and sauté with the chopped coriander in two tablespoons of ghee or butter.
- ▼ Add the okra and lemon juice to the meat and stir well.
- ▼ Stir in the coriander mixture.
- ▼ Shake, don't stir, the pot and cook the okra over low heat for 30 minutes.
- ▼ Serve hot with cooked rice.

Dried Okra Stew

Yakhnet Bamia Yabseh

- ▼ Substitute 10 oz (300 g) of dried okra for the 2 lb (1 kg) of fresh okra.
- ▼ Wash and soak in warm water for one hour.
- ▼ Prepare and cook as directed in fresh okra stew.

Karbouzeh

Karbouzeh

2 lb(1 kg) Karbouzeh
1/2 cup oil
1 big onion
1/2 cup chickpeas, cooked
4 garlic cloves
a dash salt
1 tablespoon hot chilli paste

5 persons

- ▼ Chop the onion finely.
- ▼ pick over, and remove any yellow leaves from the karbouzeh, wash well.
- ▼ Sauté the chopped onion in oil, until translucent, then add the chickpeas, and karbouzeh.
- ▼ Crush the garlic cloves with the salt and stir into the karbouzeh mixture. Add the hot chilli paste.
- ▼ Cook for 10 minutes, then serve cold with spring onions.

All Vegetable Stew
Yakhnet al Khodra

2 large eggplants
4 zucchini
4 sweet green peppers
2 cups okra
2 cups green beans (optional)
6 red tomatoes
4 small onions
6 garlic cloves
1/2 teaspoon each pepper and cinnamon
1/2 cup water
1 1/2 tablespoon salt
2 cups olive oil
1/2 cup minced green coriander

6 persons

- Peel the eggplants, onions and tomatoes.
- Cut the eggplants, onions, tomatoes and zucchini into 2 inch slices.
- Wash, cut off the ends, string and chop the beans into 1 inch pieces.
- Cut off the stems of the okra, wash and drain.
- Heat the oil and fry lightly each kind of vegetable alone and drain.
- In the base of a casserole, place a layer of eggplants.
- Top with zucchini, onions, okra then peppers and beans. Season.
- Cover with the garlic cloves, coriander and tomato slices.
- Sprinkle the water and remaining oil on top.
- Cover and cook over low heat for 1 1/2 hours.
- Leave to cool for 15 minutes, then invert the casserole over a large serving dish.
- Remove the casserole carefully and serve with roast meat or chicken.

Baked Vegetables
Khodra bil Forn

1 lb (1/2 kg) potatoes
1 lb (1/2 kg) carrots
1 lb (1/2 kg) zucchini
1 lb (1/2 kg) eggplants
2 lb (1 kg) tomatoes
4 onions
1 cup ghee
1 green sweet pepper
1 lb (1/2 kg) stewing meat, cubed
juice of one lemon
1 tablespoon salt
a dash of pepper, cinnamon

5 persons

- Peel the onions, carrots, eggplants and potatoes. Wash and chop into medium-sized pieces.
- Wash the zucchini and pepper and cut into medium-sized pieces.
- Peel and chop the tomatoes finely.
- Sauté the meat and onions in the ghee for 5 minutes then add the tomatoes, carrots, and seasoning. Cook over low heat for 20 minutes.
- Place all the vegetables and meat in an ovenproof dish and bake in a hot oven for 25 minutes.
- Serve hot.

Stuffed Turnips
Lift Mahshi

2 lb (1 kg) turnips
5 garlic cloves
2 1/2 cups water
1 cup vegetable oil for frying
1/4 cup dry tamarind paste
1/2 teaspoon salt

STUFFING
200 g minced beef
1/2 cup short grain rice, washed
1/4 cup ghee
1/2 teaspoon salt
a dash each allspice, cinnamon

5 persons

- Wash the turnips and core from one side leaving a shell, 1 cm in thickness.
- Pick over the rice, wash and drain.
- Add the seasoning and salt to the rice.
- Stir in the meat and combine well.
- Wash the turnips again from inside and outside.
- Stuff with the rice mixture, then brown a little in the oil.
- Place the dried tamarind in a pot and add 1/2 cup water. Let boil for 3 minutes over medium heat.
- Strain the tamarind juice over the fried turnips and add water to cover.
- Add crushed garlic and salt to the turnips in the saucepan and cook over gentle heat for 1 1/2 hours.
- Serve hot.

Baked Stuffed Potatoes
Mihshi Batata

4 lb (2 kg) potatoes
1 lb (1/2 kg) minced meat or lamb
1 onion, finely chopped
1/2 cup pine nuts
1/2 cup vegetable oil, for frying meat
1 teaspoon salt (for the stuffing)
1/2 teaspoon each pepper, cinnamon
1 cup vegetable oil for browning the potatoes
2 1/2 cups water
1/2 cup lemon juice
1 teaspoon salt

6 persons

- ▼ Peel and wash the potatoes.
- ▼ Make a hole on one side of the potato and scoop out the pulp, leaving a shell 1 cm thick.
- ▼ Brown the potatoes lightly in hot oil. Leave aside to cool.
- ▼ Sauté the pine nuts in half a cup of vegetable oil until golden brown. Remove and drain.
- ▼ Add the meat and onion to the remaining oil. Season and sauté for 15 minutes.
- ▼ Add the pine nuts to the above stuffing and stuff the potatoes completely.
- ▼ Arrange the stuffed potatoes in an ovenproof dish.
- ▼ Add the water, salt, lemon juice to the potatoes and bake in a hot oven for 20 minutes.
- ▼ Serve hot with cooked rice.

Fried Potatoes with Coriander
Batata bil Kozbara

3 lb (1 1/2 kg) potatoes
3 cups vegetable oil
juice of one lemon
1 1/2 cups chopped fresh coriander
5 garlic cloves
1 tablespoon salt

- Peel, wash and cut the potatoes into small cubes.
- Sauté until golden brown in hot oil. Drain.
- Crush the garlic with salt and sauté with the coriander in the remaining oil for 3 minutes.
- Add the fried potatoes to the sautéed garlic and coriander and mix well.
- Drain excess oil. Pour the lemon juice over the potatoes and serve cold.

Sweet Peppers in Oil
Fleifleh b'Zeit

4 tablespoons olive oil
1 large onion, thinly sliced
2 garlic cloves
1 lb (1/2 kg) red sweet peppers
2lb (1 kg) ripe tomatoes, peeled and chopped
salt

6 persons

- Heat the oil and brown the onions and the garlic cloves lightly.
- Remove the seeds and the meaty substances from the peppers and chop coarsely. Add to the onions and simmer, covered, over low heat for 10 minutes.
- Add the tomatoes and seasoning and cook, uncovered, for another 25 minutes.
- When the tomatoes become very soft, remove from the heat and serve hot or cold with meat or chicken.

Spinach with Minced Meat
Yakhnet el Sabanekh

2 lb (1 kg) spinach
1 lb (1/2 kg) minced meat
1/2 cup pine nuts
1/2 cup butter or vegetable oil
1 cup water
2 medium-sized onions, finely chopped
1/4 cup flour
1/4 cup butter to sauté the spinach
a dash each, pepper, cinnamon, paprika

5 persons

- Pick over and cut the tough stems from the spinach. Chop very finely and wash in several waters until it is free from soil.
- Drop the chopped spinach in boiling water and let boil for 1 minute. Drain well.
- Sauté the boiled spinach in butter for 5 minutes.
- Stir in the flour, one cup of water and a dash of salt. Simmer for 3 more minutes.
- Lightly brown the pine nuts in butter or vegetable oil.
- Remove and drain.
- Sauté the chopped onions and meat in the remaining oil.
- Add the seasonig and simmer for 15 minutes.
- Place the sautéed spinach in a saucepan and top with the browned meat and onions. Let simmer for 5 minutes.
- Garnish with pine nuts and serve hot with cooked rice.

Mashed Potatoes with Burghul

Kibbet el Batata -1-

2 lb (1 kg) potatoes
2 cups burghul
2 tablespoons flour
1 tablespoon salt or to taste
1 teaspoon each ground cumin, dried coriander, chilli and marjoram
1 cup chopped green coriander

STUFFING

3 cups onion slices
1/2 cup cooked chickpeas
1/2 teaspoon each ground dried coriander, cumin and pepper
1/4 cup sumac
3 tablespoons pomegranate syrup (rib rumman)
1/2 cup olive oil

6 persons

- ▼ Boil, peel and mash the potatoes in a vegetable grinder.
- ▼ Add the burghul and seasoning to the mashed potatoes and knead well.
- ▼ Prepare and cook as directed in mashed pumpkin with burghul.
- ▼ Bake and serve cold.

Mashed Potatoes with Burghul (-2-)

Kibbet el Batata -2-

1 lb (1/2 kg) potatoes, boiled
3/4 cup fine burghul
1/4 cup flour
1 egg
1 tablespoon salt
dash of cinnamon and black pepper
1/4 cup water

STUFFING

1/2 cup ghee or oil
1lb (1/2 kg) minced meat or lamb
1/4 cup pine nuts
1 teaspoon salt
a dash of cinnamon and black pepper
5 cups oil for frying

8 persons

- ▼ Remove the skin of the boiled potatoes and mash well or purée in a blender with the moist burghul.
- ▼ Kneed well until the potatoes and burghul become one smooth ball.
- ▼ Prepare the stuffing
- ▼ Form the burghul-potato paste into small balls, the size of a walnut.
- ▼ Flatten each ball in the palm of the hand and fill it with a tablespoon of stuffing.
- ▼ Wet the hands a little and close up the paste and reshape into a ball.
- ▼ Roll each ball in the beaten egg. Then roll in the flour.
- ▼ Brown every 4 balls in hot oil.
- ▼ Drain on paper towels.
- ▼ Serve hot.

Baked Mashed Potatoes
Batata bil Forn

6 lb (3 kg) potatoes, boiled
3/4 cup toasted breadcrumbs
2 1/2 cups milk
1 tablespoons salt
1/4 cup vegetable oil or butter,
40 cm round baking dish

STUFFING
1 lb (1/2 kg) minced meat or lamb
3 onions finely chopped
1/4 cup pine nuts
1/2 cup butter or ghee
1/4 teaspoon pepper
1 teaspoon salt
a dash of cinnamon

10 persons

- ▼ Wash and boil the potatoes. Peel and set aside to cool.
- ▼ Mash the potatoes in a vegetable strainer and knead with salt and milk until it becomes soft and smooth.
- ▼ Prepare the stuffing(*).
- ▼ Grease the baking dish with 1/4 cup oil. Sprinkle it with half the amount of the breadcrumbs.
- ▼ Wet your hands and cover the bottom of the greased dish with one inch layer of mashed potatoes.
- ▼ Cover this layer with a layer of stuffing.
- ▼ Cover the stuffing with another layer of mashed potatoes and brush the surface with a little milk.
- ▼ Sprinkle the remaining bread crumbs on top of the potato layer and bake in a hot oven for 20 minutes.

Potato Stew
Yakhnet el Batata

6 lb (3 kg) mature potatoes
2 garlic bulbs, peeled
1 cup coriander, finely chopped
10 cups water
1/2 cup lemon juice
1 lb (1/2 kg) stewing meat, cubed
3 cups vegetable oil, to fry the potatoes
1 tablespoon salt
1/2 teaspoon each, paprika and black pepper
a dash of cinnamon

10 persons

- Place the meat and the required amount of water in a pot and bring to the boil.
- Remove the scum from the water and cook, covered, over low heat for one hour.
- Peel, wash and cut the potatoes into medium-sized cubes.
  Sauté in hot oil until light brown. Drain.
- Wash and drain the chopped coriander.
- Crush the garlic cloves and sauté with the chopped coriander in a 1/4 cup of vegetable oil.
- Add the coriander mixture to the meat with the lemon juice and the fried potatoes. Season.
- Bring the pot to the boil, reduce the heat and cook for 5 minutes without stirring the potatoes.
- Serve hot with cooked rice.

Stuffed Tomatoes and Green Peppers
Mihshi al Banadoura wal Filfil

2 lb (1 kg) ripe, firm tomatoes
1 lb (1/2 kg) green sweet peppers
2 onions, finely chopped
1/4 cup pine nuts
1/2 cup ghee or butter
4 garlic cloves
13 oz (400 g) minced meat
1 teaspoon salt for the stuffing
1/2 teaspoon salt for the sauce
1/2 teaspoon each pepper, cinnamon

8 persons

- ▼ Wash and drain the vegetables.
- ▼ Sauté the onions and meat in 3 tablespoons butter.
- ▼ Season, stir well and cook for 15 minutes.
- ▼ Heat 1 cup butter and brown the pine nuts lightly. Remove from the butter and drain. Add to the meat.
- ▼ Sauté the tomatoes and peppers lightly in the remaining butter.
- ▼ Remove and arrange in an ovenproof dish.
- ▼ Using a sharp knife, cut a thin slice off the top of each tomato and pepper and remove the seeds and pulp. (Keep the tomato pulp aside).
- ▼ Stuff the peppers and tomatoes with the meat and pine nuts and replace the tops.
- ▼ Crush the garlic with the salt and mix with the tomato pulp.
- ▼ Pour this mixture over the tomatoes and pepper and bake in a hot oven for 10 minutes.
- ▼ Serve hot with cooked rice.

Tomato Stew

Yakhnet el Bonadoura

- 1 lb (1/2 kg) minced meat
- 5 onions, coarsely chopped
- 1/4 cup pine nuts
- 1/2 cup butter
- 1 tablespoon salt
- 1/2 teaspoon each pepper, cinnamon
- 4 lb (2 kg) ripe tomatoes peeled

5 persons

▼ Sauté the pine nuts in the butter until light brown.

▼ Drain and remove from the butter.

▼ Brown the meat and onions in the remaining butter.

▼ Season and cook over low heat for 15 minutes.

▼ Chop the peeled tomatoes coarsely and add to the onions and meat.

▼ Stir the mixture well and cook over low heat for 15 minutes.

▼ Serve the tomatoes garnished with pine nuts.

▼ Eat with cooked rice.

Truffles with Meat

Kima b'Lahm

13 oz (400 g) stewing meat or lamb
2 lb (1 kg) truffles
3 tablespoons butter
1/2 teaspoon salt
1/4 cup lemon juice
1/2 cup water
2 medium-sized onions, finely chopped
a dash each, cinnamon and allspice

5 persons

- ▼ Soak the truffles in water for half an hour. Scrub well with a brush and wash in several waters.
- ▼ Cut the truffles into small pieces.
- ▼ Sauté the chopped onions in butter with the seasoning.
- ▼ When the onions are soft, add the meat, salt and water. Cook over low heat for 30 minutes.
- ▼ Add the truffles and lemon juice to the meat and onion mixture and cook over low heat for 15 or 20 minutes.
- ▼ Serve hot with cooked rice

MEAT

Stuffed Lamb

Kharouf mihshi

22 lb (10 kg) young lamb prepared for stuffing at the butcher's
4 lb (2 kg) minced lamb
7 cups long grain rice
14 cups water for the rice
3 tablespoons salt
1 cup almonds
1 cup pine nuts
1 cup pistachio nuts
7 tablespoons cinnamon
7 tablespoons paprika
7 tablespoons black pepper
1 tablespoon ground nutmeg
7 tablespoons saffron
7 tablespoons ground cardamom
2 cups ghee

20 persons

- Blanche the almonds by boiling in a little amount of water. Drain and peel.
- Pick over the stones or hard stuff from the pistachio nuts and pine nuts.
- Brown the almonds in one cup ghee. When light brown, add the pine nuts and brown with the almonds. Remove and drain.
- Brown the pistachio nuts in the remaining ghee for 2 minutes. Remove and drain.
- In a large pot, place the minced lamb and one cup of ghee. Sauté with 3 tablespoons salt and one tablespoon each of paprika, saffron, black pepper, cinnamon and cardamom.
- Wash the rice in several waters and drain.
  Add the rice to the meat in the pot with 14 cups of hot water.
  Stir well and cook for half an hour over low heat.
- When cooked, remove the rice and meat from the heat. Add the pistachios, pine nuts and almonds to the rice and mix well.
- Wash the lamb from inside and outside. Wipe dry.
- Mix the seasoning in a plate and rub the inside of the lamb with half the seasoning.

  Rub the outside of the lamb with the remaining half.
- Fill the lamb with the stuffing .
  Sew the opening with a needle and thread.
- Truss the lamb by tying the hind shank with the fore shank.
- In a special large pot, place a few bay sticks and leaves on the bottom so that the lamb won't stick to the pot.
- Place the lamb in the pot and add 8 cups of water and one tablespoon salt.
- Place the pot on high heat until it comes to the boil. Reduce the heat and cover the pot tightly by plastering the cover to the pot with a piece of cloth dipped in wet dough. Cook for 5 hours.
- Remove the piece of cloth from the cover and place the lamb on a large tray or platter.
- Brown a little by baking in a hot oven for a few minutes.

Stuffed Lamb Shoulder

Al Dal'a' Al Mihshi

4 lb (2 kg) shoulder of lamb (have the butcher cut an opening on one side of the shoulder for stuffing)
3 cups of water

STUFFING

8 oz (250 g) minced beef or lamb
1 1/2 cups long grain rice
1/2 cup ghee or butter
1 tablespoon each, salt, pepper, cinnamon
1 teaspoon each, ground cardamom and saffron
a dash of black pepper
1/2 cup pine nuts
1 cup almonds, blanched and peeled
2 cups water for the rice

5 persons

- Brown the peeled almonds in the ghee. Remove and drain.
- Brown the pine nuts in the remaining ghee. Remove and drain.
- Brown the minced meat and half the amount of seasoning in the remaining butter or ghee. Add the water to the meat and allow to boil for 5 minutes.
- Wash the rice in several waters and add to the meat and hot water. Stir well, reduce the heat and cook for 25 minutes.
- Meanwhile, wash the shoulder well (inside and out) and wipe dry. Rub the shoulder with half the amount of seasoning from the inside and outside.
- Mix the rice and meat with the pine nuts and almonds.
- Fill the opening in the shoulder with this stuffing. Fasten the opening with skewers or a needle and thread.
- Brown the shoulder in butter or ghee, on both sides.
- Add three cups of water to the browned shoulder and cover the pot tightly. Bring to the boil, reduce the heat and cook for 2 hours.
- Place the shoulder on a tray and bake in a hot oven for 15 minutes.
- Pour some sauce on the shoulder and serve hot garnished with some browned almonds.

Chitterlings

Fawaregh

4 sheep chitterlings, cut and cleaned at the butchers'
1 onion, quartered
1 1/2 cups short grain rice
200 g ground beef
1/4 cup ghee or butter
1/2 cup pine nuts
1 cup flour
1 teaspoon each, salt, pepper and cinnamon

8 persons

▼ Turn the chitterlings inside out and scrape the mucous covering off completely.

▼ Wash in cold water and rub with salt and flour. Wash again.

▼ Wash the rice, drain and add it to the ground beef. Stir in the spices, ghee and pine nuts.

▼ Stuff the chitterlings with the rice mixture by pushing the stuffing in through the opening. (see picture).

▼ Place the chitterlings in a pot with 4 cups of water and the quartered onion and salt.

▼ Cook-covered-over gentle heat for one hour.

▼ When done, brown the chitterlings in a little butter or ghee.

▼ Serve hot with yoghurt.

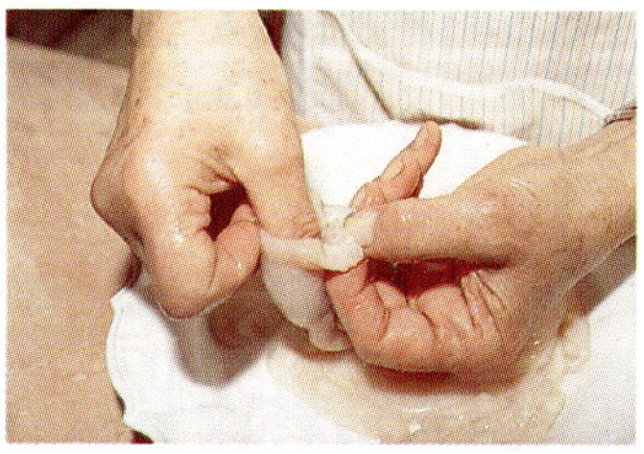

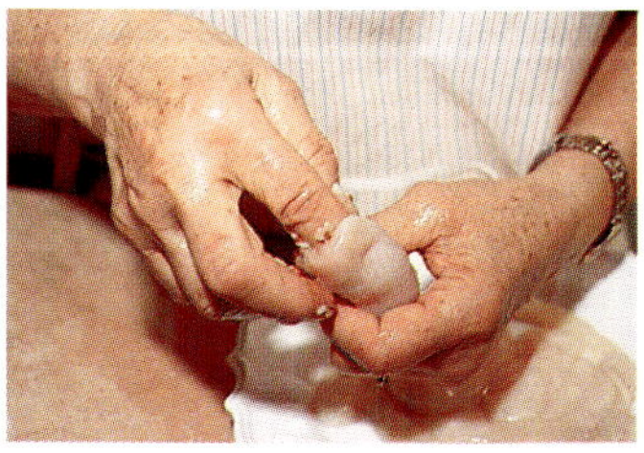

Meat on Skewers
Shish kabab

4 lb (2 kg) mutton or lamb
5 small tomatoes
1 tablespoon tomato paste
2 tablespoons lemon juice
1/4 cup olive oil
7 small onions
1 tablespoon salt
1 teaspoon each paprika, black pepper, cinnamon

10 persons

- Cut the meat into medium-sized cubes.
- Peel the onions and cut each in half.
- Marinate the meat cubes and onion halves with the oil, seasoning, tomato paste and lemon juice. Set aside for half an hour.
- On the skewers, alternate the meat cubes with the onion halves.
- Arrange the tomatoes on separate skewers, whole.
- Broil or grill about 3 inches from the source of heat. Turn to cook evenly.
- Serve hot with salad.

Stuffed Hearts
Koloub Mahshowwah

3 lamb hearts
200 g ground lamb
1/4 cup parsley, finely chopped
1/4 cup pine nuts
1 onion, finely chopped
2 tablespoons grated cheese
1/2 teaspoon salt
a dash each pepper and cinnamon
1 cup vegetable oil or butter
2 cups water plus 1 teaspoon juice of a lemon

4 or 5 persons

- ▼ Wash the hearts well, removing fat, arteries, veins and blood. Drain.
- ▼ Brown the pine nuts in half a cup of oil or butter. Remove from the oil.
- ▼ In the same oil, fry the chopped onion for 3 minutes, then stir in the ground meat. Let cook for 5 minutes.
- ▼ Add the salt and seasoning to the meat mixture. Stir.
- ▼ Stir in the parsley, cheese and pine nuts.
- ▼ Fill each heart cavity with a third of the stuffing and close the cavity by stuffing a piece of peeled potato into the opening.
- ▼ Place the remaining butter or oil in the pan and sauté the stuffed hearts in it.
- ▼ Add water and the juice of lemon to the hearts and bring to the boil.
- ▼ Reduce the heat and add a little salt, cinnamon and allspice to the liquid and cook-covered-for one hour.
- ▼ Remove the hearts from the stock.
- ▼ Brown one tablespoon of flour and stir it in the stock so as to thicken it.
- ▼ Cut each heart into slices carefully and serve garnished with tomato slice and the thickened sauce.

Roast Leg of Lamb

Fakhd Muhammar

a 5 lb (2 1/2 kg) leg of lamb
slivers of garlic
1 tablespoon salt
2 tablespoons olive oil
1 teaspoon of each ground allspice, cardamom, cinnamon, and nutmeg

8 persons

▼ Heat the oven to 400°F.

▼ Remove the whitish outer membrane from the leg of lamb and rub with the slivers of garlic and oil and spices.

▼ Insert slivers of garlic under the skin using a pointed knife.

▼ Place leg, fat side up on a rack in an uncovered greased pan. Cover pan with aluminum foil.

▼ Place the meat in a hot oven and immediately reduce the heat to 350°F.

▼ Roast the leg of lamb for 2 1/2 hours.

Meat Balls with Onions

Dawood Basha

1 lb (1/2 kg) beef
1 lb (1/2 kg) small onions
1 cup butter or vegetable oil
1 teaspoon salt
1/2 teaspoon each pepper, cinnamon
2 cups water
1 tablespoon flour
1/2 teaspoon salt
juice of one lemon or 2 tablespoons pomegranate syrup
a dash of pepper and cinnamon for broth
3 garlic cloves
1/2 teaspoon dried mint

5 persons

- Put the meat through a meat grinder twice.
- Season the ground meat and knead it with your hands. Shape into one inch balls and set aside.
- Brown the meatballs in oil. Drain and set aside.
- Peel the onions and sauté in the remaining oil until golden. Drain.
- Place the meat balls and onions in a saucepan with the water, seasoning and lemon juice.
- Bring to the boil, reduce the heat and cook for 10 minutes.
- Brown the flour in 2 tablespoons butter or ghee.
- Dissolve the browned flour in half a cup of water, stirring constantly.
- Add the dissolved flour to the meat. Let simmer for 5 minutes.
- Crush the garlic with the dried mint and add to the meat a few minutes before serving.
- Serve hot with cookedd rice.

Baked Ground Meat in Tahinah Sauce

Kafta bil Tahinah

1 lb (1/2 kg) ground beef
1 onion, large
1 cup chopped parsley
1 teaspoon salt
a dash of pepper, cinnamon

SAUCE
1/2 cup vinegar
3/4 cup tahinah
1/4 cup lemon juice
1 cup water
1 tablespoon salt
1/2 cup pine nuts

6 persons

- ▼ Peel and finely chop the onion.
- ▼ Mix the ground meat, parsley, onion and seasoning and knead well.
- ▼ Grease a round (40 cm) baking dish.
- ▼ Place the meat mixture in the baking dish and pat down until smooth and covers the bottom of the baking dish.
- ▼ In a deep dish, beat with a fork the water, vinegar, oil salt, tahinah and lemon juice.
- ▼ Pour the above sauce onto the meat and garnish with the pine nuts.
- ▼ Bake in a hot oven for 30 minutes.
- ▼ Serve hot with french-fried potatoes.

Fried Meat Fingers

Akras al Kafta al Ma'aliyyah

2 lb (1 kg) beef
1/2 teaspoon salt
1/2 teaspoon each pepper, cinnamon
1 cup vegetable oil or ghee
1 cup chopped parsley
1 onion
1/4 loaf arabic (pita) bread, moistened

6 persons

▼ Peel and coarsely chop the onion.

▼ Put the meat and chopped onion through a meat grinder twice.

▼ Mix the onion, meat, parsley, seasoning and the moistened bread. Knead the ingredients well, then put through the meat grinder, once.

▼ Knead the meat again and divide into small amounts. Shape into small fingers or patties.

▼ Heat the oil and brown the meat patties or fingers on all sides.

▼ Serve hot with cucumber and yoghurt salad.

Ground Meat with Boiled Eggs
Kafta bil Bayd

1 lb (1/2 kg) beef
5 hard-boiled eggs
1/2 cup crushed toasted breadcrumbs
1 cup ghee or butter
1 onion, small
1 egg, beaten
salt and pepper

6 persons

- Put the meat through a meat grinder twice. Add the onion to the meat grinding it once only.
- Knead the meat and onion and seasoning.
- Divide the meat into equal amounts. Wet the hands with water or a little oil and flatten each amount of meat between the hands. Place the boiled egg in the middle of the flattened meat and cover it completely with the meat. Continue this procedure until all the eggs are used.
- Dip the meat-egg balls in the beaten egg, then in the crushed breadcrumbs. Brown the meat egg balls in the butter and serve whole or cut in half.
- Garnish with tomato slices or rings.

Meat Roll with Boiled Eggs

Aleb al Kafta bil Bayd

1 lb (1/2 kg) ground meat
1 onion, large
1 teaspoon salt
a dash of pepper cinnamon
5 hard boiled eggs

5 persons

- Prepare the meat mixture as directed in "Baked Ground meat in tahinah Sauce".
- Cut out a piece of cloth (gauze) into a rectangle (25 x 30 cms). Roll out the meat with a rolling pin into a rectangle, the same size as that of the cloth.
- Place the 5 hard-boiled eggs in the middle of the meat rectangle. Leave a space of 1 inch (2 cm) at the sides.
- Begin to roll the meat loosely.
  Moisten the edge with water and plaster it down.
  Moisten the sides and pinch them together.
- Cover the meat roll with the cloth and plaster it down with water, if necessary.
- In a saucepan, large enough to fit the meat roll, add 2 cups of water and a teaspoon of salt.
  When the water comes to the boil, add the cloth covered meat roll and cook on low heat for 20 minutes.
- When the roll is well done, uncover it and set it aside to cool.
- In a large skillet, heat one cup of ghee and brown the meat roll on all sides. Remove.
  Brown one tablespoon of flour in the remaining ghee. add the browned flour to the water in which the meat roll was boiled. Bring to the boil.
- Serve the meat roll with cooked vegetables. Pour the sauce over it before serving.

Stuffed Kibbi Shells
Akras al Kibbi al Mihshiyyah

2 lb (1 kg) mutton
2 lb (1 kg) fine burghul (cracked wheat)
1 onion
2 tablespoons salt
1/2 teaspoon each pepper, cinnamon and allspice
6 cups vegetable oil

STUFFING
7 onions
13 oz (400 g) minced meat
1/2 cup ghee or butter
a dash of pepper, cinnamon
1 tablespoon salt
2 tablespoons sumac
1 cup walnuts, coarsely chopped

Makes 19 large shells or 60 very small shells

▼ Put the meat through a meat grinder twice.

▼ Remove any small stones you find in the cracked wheat and wash in several waters. Drain well .

▼ Finely chop the onion, add it to the meat and knead well. Add the seasoning, the cracked wheat and knead the meat again and put through the grinder once.

▼ Add a cup of water gradually to the meat while kneading it once more. Set aside and cover with a wet cloth.

▼ Meanwhile prepare the stuffing: chop the onions finely and sauté in the ghee with minced meat and seasoning. Cook for 15 minutes.

▼ Remove from the heat and add the sumac and chopped nuts to the stuffing. Mix well.

▼ With wet hands, mould the kibbi mixture (meat and burghul) into egg-like shapes or balls.

▼ Hold each ball in your left hand and make a hole in it with the index finger of your right hand (picture). Work your finger around the hole until a long, thin, smooth shell is formed. Keep your hand and the shell moist during the whole procedure.

▼ Fill each shell with 2 heaped teaspoons or more of the stuffing. Moisten the opening and pinch it together.

▼ Deep fry in hot oil and do not stir until 2 minutes after dropping the shells in the hot oil.

▼ Garnish the shells with mint leaves and serve hot with salad.

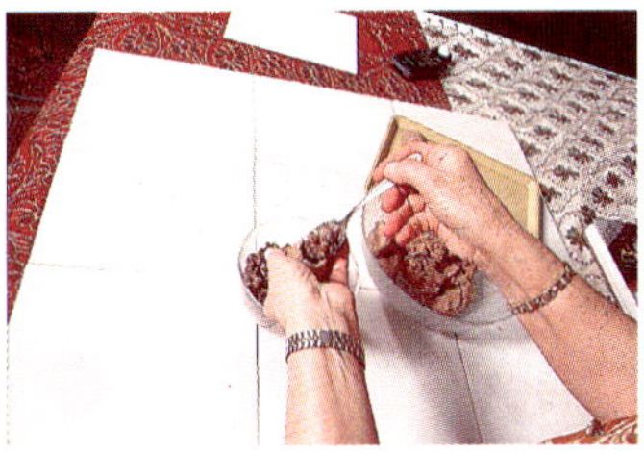

Kibbi Shells In Olive Oil

Kibbi b'Zeit

6 oz (200 g) meat (preferably mutton)
1 cup fine burghul (cracked wheat)
1 onion
1 tablespoon salt
1/2 teaspoon each pepper, cinnamon
1/2 cup finely chopped walnuts
5 garlic cloves crushed with a little salt
1 cup finely chopped parsley
1/4 cup finely chopped mint
1/2 lemon juice
1/2 cup olive oil
1/4 cup hot chilli paste

STUFFING
6 oz (200 g) minced meat
2 onions, finely chopped
1/2 teaspoon salt
a dash of paprika
a dash of black pepper
1/2 cup ghee or vegetable oil

10 persons

- ▼ Prepare the Kibbi mixture as directed in "stuffed kibbi shells" and knead it well.
- ▼ Divide it into balls and fill with the stuffing(*).
- ▼ In a pot, pour 6 cups of water and bring to the boil. Drop the shells carefully, into the boiling water. Cook for 15 minutes.
- ▼ Remove the boiled shells and place in a large platter.
- ▼ Mix the chopped walnuts with half a cup of water and add lemon juice, olive oil, chopped parsley, mint, chilli and the crushed garlic. Stir to combine.
- ▼ Pour half the amount of this sauce onto the kibbi shells and serve the remaining sauce in a separate plate.
- ▼ Serve cold.

Mashed Rice Balls with Meat

Kibbeh al Riz

2 cups rice
250 g ground lean meat
1 small onion
a dash each salt, pepper and cinnamon
1 cup diced turnips
1 cup chopped swisschard leaves
1/2 cup cooked chickpeas
1 tablespoon chopped celery leaves
juice of one lemon
salt to taste
4 cups meat broth

4 persons

- ▼ Soak the rice overnight, drain and set aside to dry.
- ▼ Grind the rice in the electric blender until fine.
- ▼ Grind the meat with the onion in the food processor. Add to the rice and seasoning.
- ▼ Place the vegetables and the juice of one lemon in a pot with the meat broth. Cover and cook for 20 minutes.
- ▼ Dampen your hands with water and knead the rice mixture until smooth.
- ▼ Form into walnut size balls.
- ▼ Drop the rice balls into the vegetable soup when it starts boiling.
- ▼ Let boil for 10 more minutes.

Kibbi in Tahinah Sauce

Kibbi Arnabiyyeh

250 g meat
1 cup burghul, fine
1 onion
1 tablespoon salt
1/2 teaspoon black pepper
1/2 teaspoon cinnamon

STUFFING
250 g minced meat
2 onions, chopped
1 teaspoon salt
a dash each pepper and cinnamon
1/2 cup ghee
1/4 cup pine nuts

TAHINA SAUCE
2 lb (1 kg) onions
2 lb (1 kg) tahinah
4 lb (2 kg) oranges
4 lb (2 kg) tangerines
1 lb (1/2 kg) lemons
4 lbs (2 kg) bitter oranges
1 tablespoon pomegranate syrup
2 tablespoons vinegar
4 cups water
2 tablespoons salt
1/2 cup vegetable oil for browning the onions

6 persons

- ▼ Prepare the Kibbi shells and arrange on a tray.
- ▼ Squeeze the oranges and tangerines and lemons.
- ▼ Strain the juice.
- ▼ Place the tahinah in a pot and add the water and juice gradually-stirring constantly-until the mixture becomes smooth and free of lumps.
- ▼ Add the salt, vinegar and pomegranate syrup.
- ▼ Brown the chopped onions in the oil, then add water to cover and let cook over low heat for 20 minutes.
- ▼ Grind the onions in a food grinder and add to the tahinah mixture.
  Stir well.
- ▼ Cook the tahinah mixture over medium heat until it comes to the boil. Cook 20 more minutes or until the sesame oil appears on the surface. Stir constantly.
- ▼ Add the kibbi shells one by one to the tahinah sauce while cooking over medium heat.
- ▼ Stir carefully with a wooden spoon.
- ▼ Let boil for 5 minutes .
- ▼ Garnish with browned pine nuts and serve with rice.

Kibbi Shells in Yoghurt
Kibbi b'Laban

6 oz (200 g) mutton
1 cup burghul (cracked wheat)
1 onion
1 tablespoon salt
1/2 teaspoon each paprika, black pepper, cinnamon

STUFFING

6 oz (200 g) minced beef
2 onions, finely chopped
1 teaspoon salt
a dash of black pepper
1/2 cup ghee or vegetable oil
1/4 cup pine nuts
3 lb (1 1/2 kg) yoghurt
1 teaspoon salt
1/2 cup short grain rice
3 garlic cloves
1cup coriander, chopped
1/4 cup ghee
dried mint

6 persons

- Prepare the Kibbi mixture, shape into shells and stuff with the stuffing(*).
- Cook the yoghurt(*).
- Boil the rice in one cup of water for 15 minutes. Add the cooked yoghurt.
- When the yoghurt comes to the boil, drop the stuffed shells carefully into it. Make sure that the yoghurt is cooking on high heat so that the shells don't stick together. Simmer for 5 minutes.
- Crush the garlic and sauté in the ghee with the chopped coriander until it becomes soft.
- Add the garlic and coriander to the yoghurt and kibbi shells. Let cook for 5 minutes.
- Serve hot or cold, garnished with a sprinkling of dried mint.

Raw Kibbi

Kibbi Nayyé

1 lb (1/2 kg) mutton
1 cup burghul (cracked wheat)
1 small onion
1 tablespoon salt
1/2 teaspoon each pepper, cinnamon, cumin
A dash basil

7 persons

- ▼ Put the meat through a grinder twice.
- ▼ Remove any stones you find in the cracked wheat and wash in several waters.
  Drain by squeezing with your hands.
- ▼ Put the onion through the grinder once.
  Knead the ground onion with the meat.
- ▼ Add the cracked wheat and seasoning to the ground meat and onion. Knead well.
- ▼ Add a little water while kneading the meat to make it soft and smooth.
- ▼ Spread the kibbi mixture on a platter.
  Garnish with onion rings and mint leaves.
- ▼ Pour a little olive oil on it and serve.
- ▼ Raw kibbi should always be eaten on the same day.
  Any leftovers should be cooked or fried.

Baked Kibbi

Kibbi bil Forn

2 lb (1 kg) mutton
1/2 teaspoon each pepper, cinnamon
1 onion
1 cup ghee
1 lb (1/2 kg) fine burghul (cracked wheat)
1/2 cup oil
1 tablespoon salt

STUFFING

10 onions, finely chopped
1 lb (1/2 kg) minced meat
1/2 cup vegetable oil
1 teaspoon salt
1/2 teaspoon each, pepper, cinnamon, sumac
1 cup pine nuts

10 persons

- ▼ Brown the pine nuts in the oil. Drain.
- ▼ Sauté the chopped onions in the remaining oil with the seasoning. Add the minced meat and sauté for 15 minutes.
- ▼ Remove the stuffing from the heat and add the pine nuts to it and mix well. Set aside.
- ▼ Remove the stones from the burghul and wash in several waters. Drain.
- ▼ Put the meat through a meat grinder and grind twice. Add the onion and grind it with the meat, once.
- ▼ Add the burghul to the meat, knead well and put the mixture through the grinder once.
- ▼ Season the ground mixture and knead well with moistened hands.
- ▼ Grease a round baking dish (40 cms) with butter.
- ▼ Divide the kibbi mixture into two equal parts. Pat one half of the mixture and smooth down until it covers the bottom of the baking dish, evenly (1 cm thick).
- ▼ Wet your hand and smooth the mixture again.
- ▼ Cover kibbi mixture with the stuffing and top the stuffing with the remaining layer of kibbi mixture. Smooth it down with wet hands until it becomes an even surface.
- ▼ Brush the oil and ghee on the kibbi mixture and make deep diagonal and horizontal lines with a sharp knife so that the oil can penetrate.
- ▼ Bake in a hot oven for 20 minutes.
- ▼ Serve hot with yoghurt and cucumber salad.

Kibbi with Sumac

Kibbi b'sumac

2 lb (1 kg) eggplants
2 lb (1 kg) tomatoes
1/4 cup sumac
500 g stewing meat with bones
1 teaspoon salt
a dash pepper

KIBBI

1 lb (1/2 kg) fine burghul (cracked wheat)
1 onion
1/2 kg lean beef
1/2 cup vegetable oil
1/2 cup pine nuts
1/2 teaspoon each, salt, cinnamon and pepper

8 persons

- ▼ Peel the tomatoes, then chop finely.
- ▼ Rinse meat then place with bones in a big pot with two cups of water.
- ▼ Place pot over high heat and bring to the boil. Remove scum, add the tomatoes and cook, covered, for 30 minutes.
- ▼ Soak the sumac in half a cup of water for 15 minutes. Strain and add the strained liquid to the meat and bones mixture.
- ▼ Add half a teaspoon of salt and a dash of pepper to the meat in the pot.
- ▼ Peel and dice the eggplants then add to the meat in the pot. Let cook for 10 minutes.
- ▼ Sauté the pine nuts in oil until golden in color. Remove from the oil.
- ▼ Prepare Kibbi (see stuffed Kibbi Shells) and stuff with pine nuts. Kibbi shells should be no bigger than an egg.
- ▼ Add the stuffed shells-one at a time-to the tomato and eggplant mixture. Do not stir.
- ▼ Bring the pot to the boil then cook over medium heat for 10 minutes.
- ▼ Serve hot with or without rice.

Kibbi with Fava Beans

Kibbi Mishimshiyyeh

1 lb (1/2 kg) green fava beans
1 lb (1/2 kg) stewing meat
1/2 cup swisschard, finely chopped
1 cup green coriander, finely chopped
4 cloves garlic, crushed
3 lb (1 1/2 kg) yoghurt
1/2 cup vegetable oil
10 prepared stuffed small Kibbi shells
1 teaspoon salt
a dash pepper
1 egg
1 tablespoon cornstarch

7 persons

- Cook the yoghurt using the egg and cornstarch: (see how to cook yoghurt(*).
- Place the meat in a pot with 2 cups water and cook covered over medium heat for 30 minutes.
- Wash the chopped coriander, drain and add to the crushed garlic and salt.
- Sauté the green fava beans in the oil over medium heat for 10 minutes. Stir in chopped swisschard and the coriander mixture.
- Add the cooked yoghurt to the meat in the pot. When it comes to the boil, add the Kibbi shells-one at a time.
- Add the fava bean mixture to the yoghurt mixture and let cook for two minutes.
- Serve hot.

Lamb in Yoghurt
Mansaf

- 4 lb (2 kg) lamb shoulder on the bone cut into even-sized pieces
- 2 lb (1 kg) yoghurt
- 2 pieces dried yoghurt (Jameed)
- salt to taste
- 1 cup almonds, blanched and peeled
- 1 cup pine nuts
- 4 slices very flat bread (Markouk)
- 4 cups short grain rice
- 1 teaspoon each black pepper, allspice, cinnamon and saffron
- 1/2 cup gee or oil

10 persons

▼ Soak the dried yoghurt overnight until it becomes crumbly. Strain and liquify in a blender.

▼ When the dried yoghurt becomes smooth, strain in a strainer.

▼ Beat the yoghurt and add to the strained yoghurt in a saucepan.

▼ Add the meat and bone pieces to the yoghurt mixture and stir over medium heat.

▼ Bring to the boil, reduce the heat and cook covered over gentle heat for one hour or until the meat becomes tender.

▼ Cut the almonds into slivers and brown in the oil. Remove from the oil and add the pine nuts and brown.

▼ Wash the rice and stir in the same oil the almonds were browned in.

▼ Add the seasoning and 6 cups hot water. Bring to the boil, reduce the heat and cook covered-over gentle heat for 30-40 minutes.

▼ Place the bread slices in the bottom of a round pan, 50 cm in diameter.

▼ Place a little rice on top of the bread slices and pour a little of the yoghurt and meat sauce.

▼ Pile the remaining rice on the bread and pour a little more yoghurt sauce.

▼ Arrange the meat pieces on the rice and garnish with the browned nuts.

▼ Serve hot with a little yoghurt sauce.

Stuffed Neck of Lamb

Ra'abeh Mahshowweh

(1 1/2 kg) boned neck of lamb prepared at butchers'
200 g ground lamb
3/4 cup long grained rice
1 cup ghee or vegetable oil
2 tablespoons pine nuts
2 tablespoons pistachios
2 tablespoons salt
1/2 teaspoon allspice
1/2 teaspoon saffron
1/2 teaspoon cinnamon
1/2 teaspoon ground cardamon
a dash black pepper
1 cup water

4 persons

- Brown the pine nuts in 1/2 cup of ghee. Remove from the ghee and add the pistachios. Brown and remove from the ghee.
- Add the ground meat and half the amount of spices to the ghee. Brown for 5 minutes then add the cup of water.
- Wash the rice, drain, and add to the meat mixture.
- Cook the rice and meat mixture covered over gentle heat for 15 minutes.
- Rub the prepared neck of lamb from inside and outside with the remaining amount of spices.
- Add the pistachios and pine nuts to the rice mixture and stir well.
- Stuff the neck well and close the opening with a needle and thread.
- Brown the neck in the remaining amount of oil. Add 3 cups of water and cover the pot.
- Bring to the boil, then reduce the heat and cook for 2 hours or until meat is tender.

Calfs Feet with Yoghurt

Fattat Ayadi

5 calf's feet, cleaned and split
2 medium size onions, quartered
1 teaspoon lemon juice
6 cups water
1 tablespoon salt
5 garlic cloves
1/4 cup vinegar
1/4 cup pine nuts
1/4 cup ghee or oil to brown the nuts
1 1/2 cups yoghurt to which 1 crushed garlic clove is added

5 persons

- Wash the cleaned and split feet with soap and water.
- Pass the feet over a high flame to remove any stray hairs.
- Wash again. Then crack the feet in several places without actually breaking the feet.
- Place the feet in a pressure cooker, bring to the boil and change the water.
- Pour clean water on the feet to cover and add the salt, lemon juice, onion pieces and 2 cinnamon sticks.
- Cook-covered-for one hour after the whistle sounds.
- Toast one and a half pita bread, after cutting into small pieces.
- Place the toasted bread pieces in a deep dish.
- Add the vinegar and 2 1/2 cups of the feet stock. Stir over gentle heat, for 2 minutes.
- Pour the garlic yoghurt over the bread pieces and arrange the feet on top.
- Garnish with the browned pine nuts.
- Serve hot.

Meat and Yoghurt Stew

Laban Immo

3 lb (1 1/2 kg) small white onions
1 lb (1/2 kg) stewing meat, cubed
4 cups water
1/2 cup vegetable oil or ghee
3 lb (1 1/2 kg) yoghurt
1/2 tablespoon salt
a dash of pepper

7 persons

▼ Peel the onions and place in a pot with the meat. Add the ghee or oil and half the amount of seasoning and sauté over low heat for 5 minutes only.

▼ Add the water to the meat and bring to the boil. Reduce the heat and cook for one hour.

▼ Cook the yoghurt(*) and add it to the meat and onions. Allow to boil for 5 minutes.

▼ Serve hot with cooked rice.

Broiled Spleen

T'halat Mashwiyyah

4 veal spleens, cleaned at butchers'
1 cup chopped parsley
2 garlic bulbs
1 hot green pepper, chopped
1/2 tablespoon salt
1/2 teaspoon allspice
1/2 teaspoon black pepper
1/4 cup vegetable oil

6 persons

- Wash the spleens and drain.
- Cut each slightly with a knife so that it forms a pocket easy to stuff.
- Crush the garlic with the salt.
- Combine the chopped parsley, crushed garlic, spices, the hot pepper and half the oil.
- Stuff each spleen with the stuffing.
- Brush the spleens with the remaining oil and place in a very hot oven for 15 minutes.
- Serve hot, cut into slices.

Kabsah with Meat

Kabsah bilahem

4 cups basmati rice
2 lb (1 kg) stewing lamb with bones
3 tomatoes, chopped
4 onions, finely chopped
1 tablespoon tomato paste
3/4 cup ghee or vegetable oil
1/2 teaspoon of each, ground cinnamon, cumin, black pepper, cardamom, cloves and dried lime or loomi
1/2 tablespoon salt
7 cups water

ONION SAUCE

3 onions, finely chopped
1/2 cup tomato sauce
1 tablespoon tomato paste
1/2 teaspoon ground cinnamon, saffron, loomi
1/2 cup vegetable oil

8 persons

- ▼ In a large pot, gently fry the onions until translucent. Add the lamb pieces and stir over medium heat, lightly browning meat.
- ▼ Add chopped tomatoes, spices, tomato paste and water stirring well to combine. Cover and simmer for 40 minutes or until the meat is tender.
- ▼ Wash rice in several waters. Drain and stir gently into pot contents.
- ▼ Simmer-covered-over gentle heat for 20 minutes.
- ▼ Prepare the sauce: Gently fry the chopped onion until translucent then add the spices, tomato sauce, salt and tomato paste.
- ▼ Cook over gentle heat until the liquid is reduced.
- ▼ Turn the rice and meat mixture onto a plate and serve with a little sauce.

Lamb Fries

Bayd el Ghanam el Makli

4 lamb fries (testicles)
1/2 cup toasted breadcrumbs
1 egg, beaten with a little vinegar
1/2 cup vegetable oil
1/2 a lemon, cut into pieces with the peel
1 teaspoon vinegar
1 teaspoon salt
1/2 teaspoon pepper
1/4 cup parsley, chopped

4 persons

- ▼ Soak the lamb fries for half an hour in enough cold water to cover. Add the lemon pieces and vinegar.
- ▼ Place the pot over high heat. Let boil then reduce the heat and simmer for 5 minutes. Remove from the heat.
- ▼ Drain and remove the skin gently. Slice each fry into 3 slices, crosswise.
- ▼ Mix the breadcrumbs, salt and pepper in a bowl.
- ▼ In another bowl, place the beaten egg and vinegar.
- ▼ Place the oil in a skillet and heat over medium heat.
- ▼ Roll each slice in the egg mixture first, then in the breadcrumb mixture.
- ▼ Brown the breaded slices in the hot oil until deep gold in color.
- ▼ Remove from the oil and serve hot garnished with parsley and lemon slices.

Osso Bucco

Mawzat bil banadoura

2 lb (1 kg) Knuckle of veal, cut into pieces at the butchers'
5 tablespoons olive oil
Flour
1 onion, finely chopped
2 garlic cloves, crushed
1 green pepper, diced
a dash each, cumin and pepper
salt to taste
1 teaspoon black peppercorns
3 cups tomato juice
Juice of 1/2 lemon

4 persons

- Dip the knuckle pieces in flour then brown in the oil.
- Add the chopped onion and pepper corns to the meat and stir until the onion is soft.
- Add the remaining ingredients and cook-covered-over gentle heat for one hour or until the meat is tender.
- Serve hot with rice.

Stuffed Tripe

Kroush Mahshowwah

3 tripe of lamb
3 1/2 cups short grain rice
4 onions
1 lb (1/2 kg) ground lamb
1 teaspoon salt
1/2 teaspoon each, ground allspice, cinnamon and cardamom
1/2 cup butter
2 cinnamon sticks

10 persons

- Wash the tripe inside out, trim and scrub well, then wash again with soap and water. Drain.
- Each tripe is cut into four pieces so as to form pockets after sewing each 3 sides with needle and thread.
- Prepare stuffing as in chitterlings and one-third stuff each pocket and saw the remaining openings.
- Press each tripe a little with the hand and prick with a fork.
- Place in a pot and cover well with water. Add 1 tablespoon salt and half a teaspoon vinegar, the cinnamon sticks and a dash of cardamom.
- Peel and quarter the onions and add to the pot. Bring to the boil over high heat.
- Reduce the heat and simmer for 2 hours over gentle heat.
- Serve hot with yoghurt.

Fried Liver

Kibed Makli

1 lb (1/2 kg) mutton liver
1/2 cup olive oil
1/2 cup chopped onion
1/2 cup chopped parsley
1/2 cup flour
1 teaspoon each, salt, black pepper and cinnamon

6 persons

- Soak the liver slices in salted water for 5 minutes. Remove the large tubes and skin and cut into half inch slices.
- Mix the flour and seasoning well.
- Coat each slice in the flour mixture.
- Fry in hot oil, taking care not to overcook. Drain and place on a plate.
- Sprinkle with chopped parsley and chopped onions.
- Serve hot immediately.

LEGUMES

Burghul with Chickpeas

Burghul bi Dfeen

2 cups coarse burghul (cracked wheat)
1/2 cup chickpeas, soaked overnight
6 small onions
6 cups water
1/2 cup ghee
1/2 cup pine nuts
1/2 cup ghee for browning the pine nuts
2 lb (1 kg) stewing meat, cubed
1/2 tablespoon salt
a dash of cinnamon, black pepper
a dash of caraway

8 persons

▼ Sauté the chickpeas, onions, and meat in half cup of ghee for 15 minutes, over medium heat.

▼ Add the water to the meat and simmer for 1/2 hour.

▼ Brown the pine nuts in half a cup of ghee. Remove and drain.

▼ Place the remaining cup of ghee in a saucepan and sauté the burghul in it for 5 minutes. Add the sautéed burghul with the ghee and seasonning to the chickpeas, meat and onions.

▼ Stir well and cook over low heat for 35 minutes.

▼ Serve hot, garnished with the browned pine nuts.

▼ Serve with yoghurt.

Burghul in Tomato Sauce
Burghul bi Banadoura

1 cup coarse burghul
3 onions finely chopped
1 teaspoon salt
a dash chilli powder
1/2 cup oil
1 lb (1/2 kg) finely chopped tomatoes
a dash each pepper and cinnamon

3 persons

- ▼ Brown the onions in hot oil for 5 minutes then add the chopped tomatoes.
- ▼ Stir in the seasoning and salt and cook for 5 minutes over low heat .
- ▼ Pick over and wash the burghul.
- ▼ Add to the tomato sauce. The burghul must be completely covered with the tomato sauce.
- ▼ If the sauce is not enough to cover the burghul, add a little water.
- ▼ Bring to the boil, then let cook for half an hour over low heat.
- ▼ Fluff with a fork and serve hot.

Green Fava Beans with Rice
Foul Akhdar b' Riz

1 lb (1/2 kg) green fava beans, shelled
1/4 cup ghee
4 onions, medium-sized
2 1/2 cups water
1 1/2 cups short grain rice
13 oz (400 g) stewing meat, cubed
1 teaspoon salt
a dash of paprika, black pepper

5 persons

- ▼ Wash the beans and drain them.
- ▼ Peel the onions and chop finely.
- ▼ Place the chopped onions and the meat in a saucepan and sauté in the ghee for 15 minutes.
- ▼ Add 2 1/2 cups of water and cook for half an hour over medium heat.
- ▼ Add the beans and seasonning to the meat and cook for 15 minutes.
- ▼ Wash the rice in several waters and add to the meat and beans. Mix well and cook over low heat for 30 minutes.
- ▼ Serve hot with yoghurt.

Couscous

1 cup chickpeas, soaked overnight
2 cups couscous
1 cup vegetable oil or butter
2 lb (1 kg) onions
2 lb (1 kg) tomatoes
1 lb (1/2 kg) zucchini
2 lb (1kg) stewing meat or knuckle of veal
1 lb (1/2 kg) pumpkin
1 teaspoon black pepper
1 teaspoon each, paprika, cinnamon
2 tablespoons salt
2 tablespoons raisins, soaked in a little water
5 tablespoons orange blossom water
a bunch of green coriander, tied with a clean thread
a dash of saffron

8 persons

- ▼ Peel and finely chop the tomatoes.
- ▼ Peel and dice the pumpkin.
- ▼ Wash and dice the zucchini.
- ▼ Peel and cut each onion into 4 pieces. Sauté in a saucepan in 1/4 cup oil with the meat for 5 minutes.
- ▼ Add 6 cups of water and bring to the boil, and remove the scum. Add the pre-soaked chickpeas, black pepper, paprika tomatos, saffron and salt. Cover and let simmer over medium heat.
- ▼ When the meat is done (35 minutes) add the above vegetables with the bunch of coriander to the meat.
- ▼ Moisten the couscous with a little water and stir in a teaspoon of salt. Place the couscous in a metallic colander, the same size as that of the meat saucepan.
- ▼ Place the couscous colander on top of the meat pot, over low heat. Stir the couscous a little, so that the steam reaches every particle of it.
- ▼ After 15 minutes, add 2 tablespoons butter and half a teaspoon of cinnammon to the couscous and stir well.
- ▼ Cover couscous with a lid and steam for 10 minutes.
- ▼ Remove the couscous colander from the top of the pot and place in a large dish. Stir in the raisins.
- ▼ Sprinkle the orange blossom water over it.
- ▼ Remove and discard the bunch of coriander and place the vegetables and meat in another dish.
- ▼ Serve hot with harissa(*) sauce.

Fava Bean Stew

Yakhnet al Foul

13 oz (400 g) stewing meat, cubed
2 lb (1 kg) fava beans
1/2 cup oil or ghee
1/2 cup green coriander, chopped
4 garlic cloves
1 1/2 teaspoons salt
1 medium-sized onion, coarsely chopped
a dash of pepper

4 persons

- ▼ Snip off the ends, string and cut the pods into medium-sized pieces. Wash and drain.
- ▼ Crush the garlic with a teaspoon of salt. Sauté the crushed garlic, chopped coriander and onion in the oil or ghee until the chopped onion becomes translucent. (5 minutes).
- ▼ Add the fava beans and meat to the above mixture and stir occasionally over low heat for 15 minutes.
- ▼ Add the seasoning and a cup of water and cook over low heat for a further 30 minutes or until tender.
- ▼ Squeeze a little lemon juice onto the beans and serve hot with cooked rice.

Pea Stew with Meat

Yakhnet Bisellah b'lahm

- ▼ Cook as you would Pea Stew in Tomato Sauce, using 4 cups of water instead of the tomatoes.
- ▼ If the peas are canned, drain them and add them to the meat and carrots 5 minutes before serving.

Boiled Green Peas

Bisellah Maslouka

1 lb (1/2 kg) young green peas
1 1/2 cups water
1/2 teaspoon lemon juice

2 persons

- ▼ Bring the water to the boil, then add the green peas and the lemon juice.
- ▼ Reduce the heat and cook, covered, for 10-15 minutes.
- ▼ When the peas are tender, remove from the heat and drain.

Green Hulled Wheat Stew

Freekeh

2 cups freekeh (green hulled wheat)
6 small white onions
6 cups water
1/2 cup vegetable oil
1/2 cup pine nuts
2 lb (1 kg) stewing meat or lamb, cubed
1/2 teaspoon each cinnamon, black pepper and salt

5 persons

- ▼ Sauté the meat and onions in hot oil over medium heat for 15 minutes.
- ▼ Add the water and seasoning to the meat, cover the pot and bring to the boil.
- ▼ Reduce the heat and let cook for 25 more minutes or until the meat is done.
- ▼ Pick over and wash the freekeh.
- ▼ Brown the pine nuts in 4 tablespoons of oil, and remove from the oil.
- ▼ Sauté the freekeh in the same oil for 5 minutes.
- ▼ Add the freekeh to the meat, stir and cover the pot. Let cook over low heat for half an hour.
- ▼ Serve the freekeh garnished with the browned nuts.
- ▼ You may substitute chicken for the meat in this recipe.

Dried Fava Beans in Oil

Foul Mdammas

1 cup dried fava beans
3 cups water
1/2 cup lemon juice
5 garlic cloves
1/4 cup parsley, chopped
1 teaspoon salt
1/2 cup olive oil

4 persons

▼ Remove any grit and stones from the beans. Wash and soak overnight in 5 cups of water and a dash of bicarbonate of soda.

▼ Wash and drain the soaked beans and place in a saucepan with 3 cups of water.

▼ Bring to the boil, reduce the heat and cook, covered, for one hour.

▼ Crush the garlic with the salt and mix in the lemon juice. Add this mixture to the beans after removing from the heat.

▼ Pour the beans in a deep dish and sprinkle with chopped parsley.

▼ Pour a little olive oil on the beans and serve hot with spring onions.

Lima Bean Stew

Yakhnet al Fasoulia

1 lb (1/2 kg) dried lima beans
4 lb (2 kg) ripe tomatoes
1 cup chopped coriander
13 oz (400 g) stewing meat, cubed
4 cups water
5 garlic cloves
1/2 cup ghee
1 tablespoon salt
1 cup coriander finely chopped
a dash of pepper, cinnamon

5 persons

▼ Remove the grit or stones from the dried lima beans. Wash and soak overnight then drain and boil in 4 cups water for 5 minutes.

▼ Peel and chop the tomatoes.

▼ Place in a saucepan and add the beans and meat.

▼ Cook for 40 minutes.

▼ Crush the garlic with the salt, sauté with the coriander in the ghee until tender.

▼ Add the coriander, garlic, and seasoning to the beans and stir for 5 minutes.

▼ Serve hot with cooked rice.

Kishk
Kishk

1 cup kishk (burghul fermented with yoghurt)
1 onion, finely chopped
7 garlic cloves
200 g ground beef
2 tablespoons ghee
3 cups water
1 teaspoon dried mint

5 persons

- Sauté the chopped onion in the ghee until slightly brown.
- Add the meat to the onion and cook, stirring for 10 minutes.
- Add the kishk and stir to combine.
- Stir in the water, and let cook for 15 minutes over medium heat.
- Just before it is done, crush the garlic and mint and stir into the kishk mixture.
- Serve hot.

Lentils with Swisschard

Adas b'Hamod

1 cup lentils
2 lb (1 kg) swisschard
7 cups water
1 garlic bulb
1/2 teaspoon dried mint
3 medium-sized onions, finely chopped
1/4 teaspoon cumin
1/4 cup lemon juice
1/2 cup vegetable oil for the onions
1 teaspoon salt
1/4 cup flour

5 persons

- Remove any grit or stones from the lentils, then wash and drain.
- Place the lentils in a saucepan with 7 cups of water. Bring to the boil, reduce the heat and simmer for 15 minutes.
- Wash the swiss chard in several waters. Chop the leaves and stalks (tender parts only).
- Add the chopped swiss chard to the lentils with the lemon juice, cumin and salt. Allow to boil for 10 minutes.
- Brown the onions in the oil. Crush the garlic with the mint and add with the onions to the lentils when they start boiling.
- Dissolve the flour in 1/4 cup water and stir into the lentils.
- Serve hot with radishes and spring onions.

Lentils with Bread

Harrak Usba'ao

1 cup lentils
5 onions, thinly sliced
2 cups green coriander, chopped
1 garlic bulb
3/4 cup lemon juice
1 teaspoon pomegranate syrup (Rib al Rumman)
1 pita bread cut into small pieces or squares
1 cup vegetable oil
1 tablespoon salt
a dash each, cumin and allspice

6 persons

- ▼ Pick over and wash the lentils.
- ▼ Place in a saucepan, add 6 cups of water and bring to the boil.
- ▼ Reduce the heat and bring to the boil again, (20 minutes), or until the lentils are a little soft.
- ▼ Brown the onion slices in half cup of oil.
- ▼ Crush the garlic cloves with a little salt.
  Sauté the crushed garlic with the chopped coriander in a saucepan in 1/4 cup oil.
  Add the salt, seasoning half the amount of sautéed coriander and half the browned onion slices to the lentils.
- ▼ Place the lentils over low heat and stir in the pomegranate syrup and the lemon juice. Let cook for 10 minutes.
- ▼ Fry the bread pieces in 1/4 cup oil over high heat until brown in color.
- ▼ Place the browned bread pieces in a big serving dish and pour the lentil mixture on top of the bread.
- ▼ Garnish with the remaining coriander and browned onion slices.
- ▼ Serve hot.

Lentils with Onions and Rice
Mdardara b' Riz

1 cup lentils
1 1/2 cups short grain rice
3 cups water
1/2 teaspoon cumin
1 teaspoon salt
5 onions, thinly sliced
1/2 cup ghee or vegetable oil

5 persons

- Remove the grit and stones from the lentils. Wash well and put in a saucepan with 3 cups of water. Bring to the boil, reduce the heat and cook for 30 minutes.
- Wash the rice well and drain.
- Add the seasoning and rice to the lentils. Stir well and simmer over low heat for 25 minutes.
- Brown the onion slices in the ghee or oil. Remove and drain and set aside. Pour the ghee over the lentils and rice, stirring carefully. Cook for 5 minutes.
- Serve in a large dish, garnished with the onion slices.
- Serve hot with yoghurt.

Lentils with Onions and Burghul
Mdardara bi Burghul

- Cook as you would Lentils with Onions and Rice using 3/4 cup burghul instead of the rice.
- Cook for 20 minutes more than in the above recipe.

Lentils with Rice

Mjaddara

1 cup lentils
5 cups water
1/4 cup rice
1 small onion, finely chopped
1/4 cup ghee
1 teaspoon salt
1/2 teaspoon cumin

4 persons

- Remove any grit or stones from the lentils, then wash and drain.
- Wash the rice in several waters. Drain.
- Place the rice and lentils in a saucepan with 6 cups of water. Bring to the boil. Reduce the heat and cook for one hour and a half.
- When the rice and lentils are cooked, put them together with the water in which they were cooked, through a strainer.
- Place the strained mixture in a saucepan over medium heat. Season.
- Brown the onion in the ghee and add it to the lentils. Simmer over low heat for 5 minutes.
- Place in a serving dish and serve cold with spring onions and radishes.

Pea Stew in Tomato Sauce
Yakhnet Bisellah bil Banadoura

4 lb (2 kg) green peas, washed
3 carrots
3 lb (1 1/2 kg) ripe tomatoes
4 garlic cloves
1/2 cup ghee or vegetable oil
13 oz (400 g) stewing meat, cubed
1 teaspoon salt
a dash of pepper, cinnamon

5 persons

- Peel the tomatoes, chop coarsely and put through a strainer.
- Wash the meat and place it in a pot with the strained tomato juice.
- Bring to the boil and remove the scum.
- Wash and scrape or peel the carrots and dice into small pieces. Add to the meat and simmer for 20 minutes.
- Peel and crush the garlic. Sauté in the oil until light brown. Add the sautéed garlic, seasoning and peas to the meat and stir well. Cook for 25 minutes over low heat.
- Serve hot with cooked rice.

Chickpeas in Yoghurt

Fattet al Hummos

1 cup chickpeas, soaked overnight
1 loaf arabic bread
1 tablespoon salt
5 garlic cloves
1/4 cup pine nuts
1/4 cup ghee
3 cups yoghurt
13 oz (400 g) coarsely minced meat
1 teaspoon salt
1/2 cup ghee for frying the meat
a dash of pepper, cinnamon
4 cups water

5 persons

- Place the pre-soaked chickpeas in a saucepan, add water to cover and cook-covered-for one hour.
- Toast the Arabic bread in the oven, until golden. Break into small pieces.
- Crush the garlic with the salt.
- Brown the pine nuts in 1/4 cup ghee. Remove and drain.
- Brown the meat in the remaining ghee and season.
- In a round (30 cm) serving dish, place the toasted bread pieces.
- Mix the crushed garlic and the chickpeas well. Add to the bread pieces and mix well.
- Pour the yoghurt over the chickpeas and bread. Garnish the dish with the browned meat and pine nuts.
- Serve immediately.

Chickpeas in Oil
Hummos Mosabbah

1 cup dried chickpeas
1/4 teaspoon bicarbonate of soda
4 cups water
1 teaspoon salt
4 garlic cloves
1/2 cup olive oil

8 persons

- ▼ Remove any stones you might find in the chickpeas and soak overnight with the bicarbonate of soda, in a quantity of water that is almost 3 times that of the chickpeas.
- ▼ On the following day, drain the chickpeas and put in a saucepan with 4 cups of water.
- ▼ Bring to the boil and remove any foam that may have formed on the surface.
- ▼ Cook, covered, on low heat for 1 1/2 hours or until tender.
- ▼ Crush the garlic with the salt. Add to the chickpeas and mix well.
- ▼ Serve hot in a deep bowl. Pour a little olive oil on it and eat with spring onions.

Moughrabiyya

Moughrabiyya

2 chickens, drawn and cleaned
8 cups water
1 cup chickpeas, soaked overnight
1/2 cup ghee
2 teaspoons each salt, caraway, cinnamon
1 teaspoon allspice
3 lb (1 1/2 kg) white small onions, peeled
2 lb (1 kg) fresh moughrabiyya
2 tablespoons flour

10 persons

- ▼ Place the chikens in a large pot wih 8 cups of water. Bring to the boil.
- ▼ Remove the scum, reduce the heat and add the onions, chickpeas and half the amount of seasoning. Cook for 40 minutes.
- ▼ Place the moughrabiyya in a metallic colander as big as the chicken pot.
- ▼ Place the colander on top of the chicken pot and stir so that the steam will reach all the moughrabiyya particles (15 minutes).
- ▼ Remove the moughrabiyya from the colander and place in a saucepan with the ghee.
- ▼ Sauté over medium heat for 15 minutes.
- ▼ Add a little amount of chicken broth to the moughrabiyya and stir until tender. Add the remaining amount of seasoning.
- ▼ Remove the chicken from the broth, bone the chicken and cut into medium-sized pieces.
- ▼ Dissolve the flour in 1/4 cup water and stir into the meat broth and boil for 5 minutes.
- ▼ Strain the broth and pour in a tureen. Add the onions and chickpeas to the Moughrabiyya and stir carefully.
- ▼ Serve the Moughrabiyya in a large platter garnished with the onions and chickpeas, and chicken slices.
- ▼ Pour a little of the broth over it before serving.

PIES & PASTRIES

Cheese Pastry Rolls

Ra' a bi Jibn

400 g white salted cheese
1/2 cup finely chopped parsley
1/2 cup gruyère cheese, grated
300 g filo pastry
1/2 cup butter or ghee
1 cup milk

22 Rolls

- Grate the white cheese and mix it with the chopped parsley.
- Add the grated gruyère cheese to the above and mix well.
- Combine the ghee and milk in a large bowl. Fill the filo pastry as you would Meat Pastry Rolls.
- Bake in a hot oven until golden and serve hot.

Meat Pastry Rolls
R'aa' b' Lahm

200 g minced meat
1 small onion, finely chopped
1/4 cup pine nuts
1/4 cup ghee
1/2 teaspoon salt
a dash pepper, cinnamon
1 teaspoon sumac
1/2 cup gruyère cheese, grated
300 g filo pastry
1/2 cup ghee
1 cup milk

22 Rolls

- Brown the pine nuts in the ghee (1/4 cup). Remove and drain.
- Sauté the onion in the remaining ghee until soft. Add the minced meat and seasoning and sauté all the ingredients for 15 minutes.
- Remove the skillet from the heat and add the grated cheese, sumac and pine nuts to the meat mixture. Combine well.
- Mix 1/2 cup of ghee with the milk in a large bowl.
- Brush a large tray with a little milk and ghee mixture. Place a layer of filo pastry on this mixture. Cut the pastry into strips or squares and brush each square with a little ghee and milk.
- Fill each square with one teaspoon filling. Roll up firmly like a cigarette (picture).
- Arrange the rolls in well-greased trays and bake in a hot oven for 20 minutes or until golden.
- Serve hot.

Spinach Turnovers
Fatayer bi Sabanekh

1 cup water
6 cups plain flour
1 cup milk
1/2 cup vegetable oil
1/2 teaspoon salt
1/4 cup water, to moisten hands while kneading

STUFFING
4 lb (2 kg) fresh spinach
10 onions
1/3 cup sumac
1/3 cup lemon juice
1/3 cup olive oil
2 tablespoons salt

70 pieces

- Prepare and knead the dough as you would Meat Pie Pastry. Let the dough stand for one hour before stuffing.
- Meanwhile, finely chop the spinach leaves and wash in several waters. Drain.
- Chop the onions and add the salt. Set aside for 5 minutes.
- Squeeze out excess water from the spinach.
- Squeeze out the onions and add to the spinach.
- Add the sumac, olive oil, lemon juice to the spinach mixture and mix well. Add more salt, if needed.
- Divide the dough into several balls, and roll out each ball to a thickness of 2 mm onto a floured marble table.
- Cut the rolled out dough into squares.
- Fill each square with one tablespoon of filling and secure edges together by folding them over and pressing firmly together.
- Place in well-oiled baking trays and bake in a hot (350°F) oven for 20 minutes.
- Serve cold.

Cheese Trianles

Sambousek b'jibn

1 package ready made phyllo strips
1 cup grated white cheese
1/2 cup parsley, finely chopped
1 teaspoon lemon juice
1/2 cup grated gruyere cheese
1 tablespoon sesame seeds

22 triangles

▼ Mix all the ingredients except the phyllo strips.

▼ Spread each strip and stuff each strip with one tablespoon of stuffing.

▼ Roll each strip into triangles.

▼ Cover the rolls-as you make them-as they dry easily.

▼ Deep fry in hot oil until golden in color.

▼ Serve hot.

Meat Triangles

Sambousek bilahm

1 package phyllo pastry strips
1 lb (1/2 kg) minced beef
1 tablespoon sumac
1 onion, finely chopped
2 tablespoons parsley, finely chooped
1/4 cup oil
salt to taste
a dash each allspice, cinnamon

22 Rolls

- ▼ Sauté the onions in oil for 2 mintues, then stir in the minced meat.
- ▼ Cook for 10 minutes.
- ▼ Add the seasoning and parsley to the stuffing.
- ▼ Stuff each strip with one tablespoon of stuffing.
- ▼ Roll each strip so as to form triangles.
- ▼ Deep fry in oil until golden in color.
- ▼ Serve hot.

Meat Pancakes

Lahm b' Ajeen ma' a Banadoura wa Jibn

1 cup all purpose flour
1 1/2 cups milk
4 eggs
1 onion, finely chopped
1/4 cup butter or oil
12 oz (1/2 kg) minced meat
1 tablespoon chopped parsley
1/2 tablespoon each, cinnamon and pepper
1 tablespoon flour
1 teaspoon salt
1 cup milk
1 egg

SAUCE

2 cups finely minced tomatoes
1/2 cup parmesan cheese

8 persons

▼ Sift the flour and salt. Add the eggs to the flour and mix well.

▼ Add the milk to the batter and mix with a wooden spoon for 5 minutes.

▼ Cover the batter and refrigerate for 2 hours.

▼ Sauté the minced onion in butter for 5 minutes. Add the minced meat and sauté for another 5 minutes.

▼ Season the stuffing, add the parsley and let simmer over low heat for 10 minutes.

▼ Add one tablespoon flour to one cup milk and one egg and beat well. Add it to the stuffing and stir over low heat for 3 minutes.

▼ Heat a heavy frying pan (15 cm) and grease with a few drops of oil.

▼ Add a small quantity of batter (2 tablespoons), tip the frying pan and let the batter spread over the bottom.

▼ Cook the pancake over moderate heat. When it is brown underneath, turn it over and brown the other side.

▼ Remove to an ovenproof dish. Repeat the process, adding oil to the frying pan, until all are done.

▼ Fill each pancake with 2 tablespoons stuffing and roll up. Arrange pancakes in rows in a greased ovenproof dish.

▼ Pour tomatoes on top of the pancakes and sprinkle with parmesan cheese.

▼ Bake in a hot oven for 15 minutes. Serve hot.

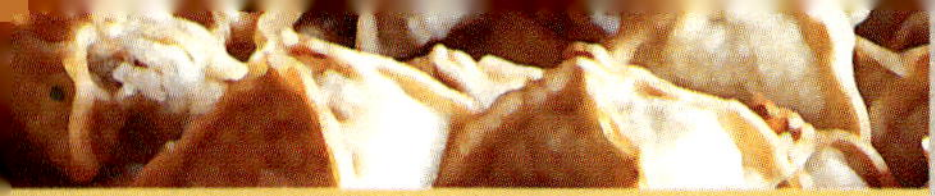

Meat Pies in Yoghurt
Shishbarak

2 cups plain flour
1 cup milk
1 cup flour for rolling out the dough
a dash salt

STUFFING
1lb (1/2 kg) mutton, finely minced
2 onions, finely chopped
1/2 cup ghee or butter
1/4 cup pine nuts
1 teaspoon salt
a dash of pepper, cinnamon
1 tablespoon parsley, finely chopped
1 tablespoon dried mint

THE YOGHURT
2 lb (1 kg) yoghurt
2 tablespoons cornflour dissolved
in 1/2 cup water
1 egg
1 tablespoon salt
3 garlic cloves

10 persons

- ▼ Sift the flour with the salt. Then mix with the milk to form a dough.
- ▼ Knead the dough for 10 minutes. If the dough is too thick and dry, moisten your hands a little.
- ▼ Set the dough aside for half an hour.
- ▼ Brown the pine nuts in the ghee or butter. Remove and drain.
- ▼ Sauté the minced meat and chopped onions in the remaining ghee or butter. Season and cook for 15 minutes.
- ▼ Remove the meat mixture from the heat. Add the pine nuts and chopped parsley and mix well.
- ▼ Roll out the dough on a large pastry board or marble table, after sprinkling a little flour first.
- ▼ Roll the dough thinly and using a biscuit cutter or coffee cup, cut into circles about 3 cm in diameter.
- ▼ Place a teaspoon of the filling on one side of the circle, then fold the other side of the circle over the top, pressing the ends together to form a crescent-shaped pie. Sprinkle one cup of flour on a large tray and arrange the crescent- shaped pies on it. Let stand for a while.
- ▼ Cook the yoghurt(*) using the quantities stated in this recipe. When it comes to the boil drop each crescent-shaped pie into the yoghurt. Cook the yoghurt with the pies for 10 minutes.
- ▼ Crush the garlic with the dried mint and add to the yoghurt one minute before serving.
- ▼ Serve hot with cooked rice.

Meat Pie Pastry
Sfiha

6 cups plain flour
2 cups lukewarm yoghurt
1/2 cup olive oil
1/2 teaspoon salt
1/4 cup warm water for moistening the hands
4 teaspoons yeast dissolved in 1/2 cup warm water

25 pies

▼ Dissolve the yeast in the water and set aside. Then sift the flour onto a pastry board or marble table top. Add the salt to the flour, mix well and make a well in the middle.

▼ Mix the yoghurt, olive oil and dissolved yeast and pour into the well. Work the dough lightly.

▼ Knead the dough well for 20 minutes. Moisten the hands while kneading to make the dough smoother and non sticky.

▼ Brush the ball of dough with a little oil. Place in a bowl and cover with a piece of cloth. Let stand in a warm place until it is almost double in size.

▼ Knead the dough for 2 minutes and divide into small balls. Cover the balls with a piece of cloth.

Meat and Pine Nut Pies

Sfiha b' Lahm wi Snoobar

1 recipe Meat Pie Pastry
1 lb (1/2 kg) minced beef
4 large onions, finely chopped
1/2 cup ghee or vegetable oil
1/2 teaspoon pepper
1/2 teaspoon cinnamon
3/4 cup yoghurt
2 tablespoons tahinah
2 tablespoons vinegar
1/2 cup pine nuts
5 firm, ripe tomatoes, seeded and chopped
1 tablespoon salt and a dash black pepper

25 pieces

- ▾ Sauté the onions and meat in the ghee for 5 minutes only. Stir in the salt and seasoning.
- ▾ Mix the yoghurt with the tahinah and vinegar. Add the chopped tomatoes and mix well.
- ▾ Add the meat and onion mixture to the tomatoes and tahinah. Combine well.
- ▾ Roll out each of the 25 dough pies into the size of a tea saucer and the thickness of 1/2 cm
- ▾ Arrange the dough circles on oiled trays or baking dishes.
- ▾ Flute the edges of the dough circles with your fingers and fill each with 2 tablespoons of filling. Sprinkle a few pine nuts on top of each pie.
- ▾ Let stand for 30 minutes after filling.
- ▾ Bake in a hot oven for 15 minutes or until golden.
- ▾ Serve hot with yoghurt.

DESSERTS

Dough Balls in Syrup

Awwamat

4 cups plain flour
1/2 cup cornflour
3 cups water
5 cups vegetable oil
2 teaspoons yeast dissolved in 2 tablespoons warm water
a dash salt

ATTER (SYRUP)
1 1/2 cups water
3 tablespoons orange blossom water
3 drops of lemon juice
5 cups sugar

10 persons

- ▼ Dissolve the yeast and set aside for 10 minutes.
- ▼ Sift the flour and the salt in a big bowl. Add the water, and dissolved yeast and mix well.
- ▼ Beat the batter with your hand until it becomes pliable and smooth.
- ▼ Cover the batter with a piece of cloth and let stand in a warm place for 4 hours, until it is double in bulk.
- ▼ Beat the batter with your hand every once in a while to prevent any bubbles from forming.
- ▼ Prepare the Atter(*) (syrup).
- ▼ Heat the oil in a heavy saucepan.
- ▼ Scoop out a little dough-enough to fill your hand-and squeeze your fist hard so as to push a ball of dough between thumb and finger.
- ▼ Scoop out the ball with a wet teaspoon and drop into the hot oil.
- ▼ The balls will swell and float to the top. Stir the balls until they are golden and crisp.
- ▼ Remove the balls from the oil, drain and drop into the cool syrup.
- ▼ Remove promptly and serve hot or cold.

Wheat in Sweet Sauce

Snooniyeh

1 cup hulled wheat
5 cups water
1 cup sugar
1/2 cup orange blossom water
1/2 cup pine nuts
1/2 cup walnuts
1/2 cup almonds, blanched, peeled, and slivered
1 cup pomegranate seeds

10 persons

- Pick over, wash and soak the wheat in water overnight. Drain.
- Place the wheat in a pressure cooker with 5 cups of water.
- Cook-covered-over medium heat until the whistle sounds. Reduce the heat and cook for an additional 1/2 hour.
- Soak the walnuts in hot water. Drain and chop.
- Soak the pine nuts in water.
- Let the pressure cooker cool down, then open it.
- Stir in the sugar until dissolved, over gentle heat.
- Remove the pot from the heat and add all the other ingredients.
- Serve hot or cold.

Pancakes with Cream

Atayef bi Ashta

3 cups atter (syrup)
1 lb (1/2 kg) small atayef store-bought
1 lb (1/2 kg) kashta (home-made cream)
1/2 cup crystallized flowers store-bought

33 pancakes

- Fill each pancake with a tablespoon of kashta.
- Pinch the edges together only half way, forming a cone-like shape.
- Garnish each pancake with a little amount of crystallized flowers.
- Arrange in a large serving dish.
- Serve with the atter.

Cheese Pancakes

Atayef b'jibn

(ATTER) SYRUP
4 cups sugar
1 cup water
1/2 teaspoon lemon juice
1/4 cup orange blossom water
1 lb (1/2 kg) unsalted white cheese
3/4 cup ghee or butter
2 lb (1 kg) medium-sized atayef store-bought

32 pancakes

- ▼ Chop the cheese into fine pieces and soak in water. If the cheese is salted, soak and change the water every 1/4 of an hour, until the cheese becomes sweet. Drain well.
- ▼ Fill each pancake with one tablespoon cheese.

  Fold into half circles and pinch the edges together to secure.
- ▼ Brush each pancake with ghee and arrange in a baking sheet or pan.
- ▼ Bake in a hot oven until light gold in color.
- ▼ Dip the stuffed pancakes in hot syrup(*) (prepared using the quantities listed). Remove and serve hot.

Ashta or Home Made Cream
Ashta

3 cups powdered milk
1/4 cup plain flour
4 cups water

- Mix the milk, flour and water in a saucepan. Place over medium heat, stirring constantly.
- Allow the milk to boil for one minute, then pour in a shallow tray or dish.
- Let stand for 2 minutes then remove the thick layer or patches of cream that have formed on the top. Keep them in a separate dish.
- Keep on removing the thick patches of cream, as they form.
- Use this cream as a filling for "Knaafeh" or "Aish al Saraya".

Home Made Cream -2-
Ashta

1/2 loaf toast bread (15 slices)
2 cups powdered milk
3 cups water
1/4 cup orange-blossom water

1 kg

- Dissolve the milk in the water and let boil over medium heat.
- Remove the outside crust from the bread.
- Crumble the bread and add to the milk.
- Stir over low heat and bring to the boil.
- Add orange-blossom water and stir well.
- Remove from the heat . The cream should have the consistency of yoghurt.
- Cover with wax paper and place in the refrigerator.

Walnut Pastry

Baklawa

2 cups butter, unsalted
17 sheets of phyllo pastry
4 cups walnuts, ground and mixed with
1 cup sugar
1/2 cup ground pistachios
4 cups sugar syrup(*) (atter)

8 persons

- Melt the butter over gentle heat.
- Brush an ovenproof deep rectangular pan with butter.
- Place one sheet of phyllo and brush with butter. Place another sheet on top and brush with butter.
- Repeat until you have 7 greased phyllo sheets.
- Spoon the walnut stuffing on top of sheet, cover with another sheet and brush with butter.
- Repeat this procedure until all the phyllo sheets are used.
- Wipe the last sheet with a little water then brush with butter and cut into the desired shapes (lozenges).
- Place the pan in a hot oven (325°F) for 20 minutes. Raise the temperature for the last 5 minutes until the Baklawa becomes golden in color.
- Remove from the oven and pour the cold sugar syrup on it.
- Garnish with pistachios.

Milk Pudding with Cornflour
Mouhallabiyya b'Nasha (1)

- 6 cups milk
- 1 cup cornflour
- 1 cup sugar
- 1/2 cup water
- 1/2 cup orange blossom water
- 3 cups peach compote
- 1 cup pine nuts
- 1 cup peeled, slivered almounds

10 persons

▼ Dissolve the cornflour in water and add to the milk. Bring to the boil, stirring constantly. Reduce the heat and cook 20 minutes, stirring constantly.

▼ Stir in the sugar and simmer for 5 minutes.

▼ Remove from the heat and add the orange blossom water.

▼ Pour the pudding into a large glass dish and set aside to cool.

▼ Meanwhile place the compote in a deep bowl with the washed pine nuts and slivered almonds.

▼ Serve the pudding in small dishes and pour some peach compote onto it.

Milk Pudding with Cornstrach
Mouhallabiyya b'Nasha (2)

- 6 cups milk
- 1 cup sugar
- 1/2 cup cornstarch
- 1/2 cup water
- 1/2 cup orange blossom water
- 1/2 teaspoon mistica pieces (gum arabic)
- 1/2 cup finely chopped pistachios
- 1/2 cup crystallized flowers

8 persons

▼ Dissolve the cornstrach in the water and strain into a saucepan. Add the milk to the strained cornstarch and bring to the boil, stirring constantly with a wooden spoon.

▼ Reduce the heat and cook for 20 minutes, stirring constantly. Add the sugar and stir.

▼ Crush the gum arabic with 1 tablespoon sugar and stir into the milk. Cook for 5 more minutes.

▼ Add the orange blossom water to the milk and remove from the heat.

▼ Serve cold in small plates garnished with pistachios and crystallized flowers.

Milk Pudding with Sugar Syrup

Ashtalliyah

6 cups milk
1 cup cornflour
1/2 cup water
1/4 cup sugar
1/4 cup rosewater
1/4 cup orange blossom water

ATTER (SYRUP)
2 cups sugar
1/2 cup water
1/2 teaspoon lemon juice
1/4 cup orange blossom water

10 persons

- ▼ Prepare milk pudding with syrup exactly as you would Milk Pudding with Cornflour.
- ▼ Pour the milk pudding into small plates to cool.
- ▼ Prepare the atter(*) using the quantities listed. Cool.
- ▼ Pour 3 tablespoons syrup over each plate and serve.

Milk Pudding with Oranges
Mouhallabia bil Burtukal

5 cups milk
1 cup sugar
1/2 cup orange blossom water
1 cup peeled, slivered almonds
3/4 cup cornstarch, dissolved in 1/2 cup water

ORANGE SAUCE
4 lb (2 kg) oranges or 3 1/2 cups orange juice
1/2 cup cornstarch
1 1/2 cups sugar

10 persons

- Dissolve the cornstarch in water. Strain into a saucepan and add the milk.
- Bring to the boil, stirring constantly for 15 minutes. Add the sugar and orange blossom water and stir for another 5 minutes.
- Remove from the heat and set aside.
- Meanwhile, prepare the orange sauce: Dissolve the cornstarch in 1/2 a cup of water.
- Squeeze the oranges and place the juice in a saucepan. Add the dissolved starch and stir over medium heat. Add the sugar, stirring constantly. Bring to the boil, and simmer for 5 minutes.
- Prepare small serving plates and pour the orange sauce into each to a depth of 1 1/2 cm only.
- Sprinkle some slivered almonds, then top with the milk pudding. Set aside to cool.
- Turn the pudding onto dessert plates, so that the orange layer is uppermost.
- Serve cold.

Apricot Paste with Cornflour

Amareddine binnasha

1 lb (1/2 kg) dried apricot paste
4 cups water
1 cup cornstarch or (3/4 cup cornflour)
1 cup sugar
1 cup almonds, blanched, peeled and slivered

8 persons

- ▼ Soak the dried apricot paste overnight in 4 cups of water.
- ▼ Strain the dissolved apricot paste in a strainer over a pot.
- ▼ Dissolve the cornstarch in 1/2 a cup of water and add to the strained apricot.
- ▼ Stir in the sugar and combine well with the cornstarch and apricot syrup.
- ▼ Place the pot over medium heat, stirring all the time. Bring to the boil, and let boil for 10 minutes.
- ▼ Remove from heat and pour into little cups.
- ▼ Garnish with almond slivers.

Plain Rice Pudding

Riz b'Haleeb

3/4 cup short-grain rice
8 cups milk
1 cup sugar
1/2 cup orange blossom water
1/2 cup finely chopped pistachio nuts
1/2 teaspoon Mistica pieces

10 persons

- Wash the rice in several waters and soak in hot water for 1 hour.
- Place the rice in a saucepan with one cup of water over medium heat. Boil for 10 minutes. Add the milk and stir constantly for 3/4 of an hour.
- Stir in the sugar. Crush the mistica (gum arabic) with one tablespoon sugar and add with the orange blossom water to the milk and rice. Remove from the heat.
- Serve cold in small platters, garnished with ground pistachio nuts.

Milk and pastry pudding

Om Ali

5 sheets filo (phyllo pastry)
3/4 cup raisins
1 1/4 cup cream
2 1/2 tablespoons butter, melted
4 cups milk plus 1 teaspoon vanilla essence
3/4 cup blanched, peeled and slivered almonds
4 tablespoons sugar

6 persons

- Brush the filo sheets with the melted butter and bake in a pre-heated oven, loosely one on top of the other for 4 minutes or until golden.
- Break the filo sheets into medium pieces and place in a deep baking dish (glass or earthenware).
- Sprinkle the raisins and almonds over the filo and set aside.
- Heat the milk and sugar and bring to the boil.
- Remove from the heat and stir in the cream and pour over the filo so that the milk covers the filo completely.
- Bake for 15 to 20 minutes or until browned.
- Serve hot.

Caraway Rice Pudding

Moughli

2 cups powdered rice
3 1/2 cups sugar
14 cups water
3 tablespoons caraway powder
1 tablespoon cinnamon
1 cup coarsely chopped walnuts soaked in cold water
1 cup pine nuts soaked in cold water
1 cup pistachios, blanched, peeled and soaked in cold water
2 cups finely grated coconut

15 persons

- Combine the rice, sugar, caraway and cinnamon.
- Place the above mixture in a large pressure cooker.
- Pour the water into the pressure cooker and cook over moderate heat stirring constantly, with a wooden spoon.
- Bring to the boil, cover the pressure cooker and place the whistle on the cover.
- When the pressure cooker starts "whistling", reduce the heat and cook for an additional hour.
- Remove from the heat and place the pressure cooker under running tap water to cool.
- Remove its cover and place over low heat stirring constantly with a wooden spoon for 20 minutes.
- Pour the pudding in small pudding cups or large plates as needed.
- Drain the nuts.
- Garnish the pudding with the grated coconut first, then top with the nuts.
- Serve cold.

Baked Rice Pudding

Ashtalliyeh bil Forn

6 cups milk
1 cup short-grain rice
2 cups toasted breadcrumbs
1 cup butter
1/4 cup orange blossom water
4 small pieces mistica (gum-arabic)

ATTER (SYRUP)

5 cups sugar
1 1/2 cups water
1/4 cup orange blossom water
1/2 teaspoon lemon juice

10 persons

- ▼ Wash the rice in several waters. Place in a saucepan with hot water to cover. Let stand for 3 hours.
- ▼ Drain the rice and grind or cream in the blender.
- ▼ Place the milk in a pot over medium heat. Add the creamed rice gradually, stirring constantly with a wooden spoon, for 1 hour.
- ▼ When the milk thickens, crush the gum arabic with a tablespoon sugar and stir into the milk. After 5 minutes, remove from the heat and set aside.
- ▼ Grease a baking dish (25 x 45 cms) with low sides, with the butter and sprinkle one cup crushed crumbs onto the bottom to cover completely.
- ▼ Gradually pour the milk into the baking dish to a height of 1 1/2 cms .
- ▼ Flatten the top of the milk with a wet spoon. Sprinkle the remaining cup of crushed crumbs on the milk to cover it completely.

- ▼ Pour 1/2 a cup of melted butter on top of the crushed crumbs and bake in a hot oven for 10 minutes only. Set aside to cool.
- ▼ Cut into squares. Pour the syrup(*) on it and serve hot or cold.

Turmeric Rice Pudding
Moufattaka

2 lb (1 kg) tahinah
10 cups water
4 lb (2 kg) sugar
1/2 cup turmeric powder
1/2 tablespoon cinnamon
2 lb (1 kg) short grain rice
1 cup pine nuts

40 persons

- Pick over and wash the rice in several waters then soak in warm water for 1 hour.
- Drain the rice and place in a pressure cooker with the turmeric and 10 glasses of water.
- Cook over high heat stirring occasionally.
- When the rice starts boiling, cover the pressure cooker and place the whistle on the lid.
- When the pressure cooker starts "whistling", reduce the heat and cook for an additional half hour.
- Open the pressure cooker after cooling it first by pouring tap water on it.
- Add the sugar, tahinah and cinnamon to the rice and stir well with a wooden spoon.
- Return the pressure cooker to the stove and place over moderate heat stirring occasionally until the mixture starts boiling.
- Cover the pressure cooker and place the whistle on the lid, then reduce the heat and cook for 2 hours.
- Remove from the heat, cool the pressure cooker by pouring some tap water on it then open and stir well with a wooden spoon.
- Return to the heat and cook on low heat for half an hour stirring constantly.
- When the pudding becomes almost one lump and the oil floats on the surface remove from the heat and stir in the pine nuts.
- Pour the pudding into large plates smoothing the heavy mixture with a spoon.
- Serve cold.

Turmeric Cake

Sfoof

3 cups fine semolina
1 cup plain flour
4 tablespoons turmeric
4 tablespoons powdered milk
1 cup vegetable oil
2 cups sugar
2 cups water
3 teaspoons baking powder
1/4 cup tahinah
1/2 cup pine nuts

15 persons

- ▼ Mix the semolina, flour, turmeric, milk and baking powder well.
- ▼ Dissolve the sugar in the water. Then add with the oil to the flour mixture. Beat well for 5 minutes.
- ▼ Grease the baking pan with tahinah (bottom and sides). and pour the batter gradually into the pan. Garnish with pine nuts and bake in a hot oven for 20 minutes.
- ▼ Remove the cake from the oven. Let it cool before cutting it with a sharp knife.
- ▼ Serve with tea.

Semolina Cake
Basbousa

1/2 cup unsalted butter
3/4 cup castor sugar
1 teaspoon vanilla essence
2 eggs
2 cups fine semolina
1 teaspoon baking powder
1/2 teaspoon bicarbonate of soda
3/4 cup yoghurt
almonds, blanched and slivered

ATTER (SYRUP)
1 1/2 cups water
3 tablespoons orange blossom water
3 drops lemon juice
5 cups sugar

10 persons

- Cream the butter, sugar and vanilla until light and fluffy.
- Add the eggs, one at a time and beat well.
- Sift the semolina, baking powder and soda. Fold into butter mixture alternately with yoghurt.
- Pour the batter into a greased 20 X 30 cms baking tray and garnish with the almonds.
- Bake in a hot oven for 30 minutes.
- Pour atter (syrup) over hot cake and let cool thoroughly.
- Cut into diamond shapes and serve cold.

Semolina and Date Cake

Makrouta

2 cups atter* (sugar syrup)
2 cups flour
4 cups semolina
1/2 cup melted butter
2 cups vegetable oil
1 cup water
1/2 teaspoon mahlab (a spice found in middle Eastern shops)
1/4 cup each orange blossom and rose water
2 tablespoons yeast dissolved in 1/2 cup warm water

FILLING
5 cups seeded soft dates
1/4 cup butter
1/2 cup sesame seeds

25 persons

- Mix the semolina and flour in a pan, stir in the melted butter and oil and mix with your fingers until crumbly.
- While kneading with your fingers, sprinkle the dissolved yeast and rose and blossom water over the semolina mixture and mix well.
- Cover the semolina and set aside in the fridge for one hour.
- Pre-heat the oven to 350°F.
- Knead the dates with the butter until soft and smooth.
- Divide the semolina dough into two equal parts.
- Grease a round (35 cm diameter) pan with butter.
- Place one half of the semolina dough on the bottom of the pan and pat until smooth and flat.
- Place the date dough between two wax sheets and flatten with a rolling pin to a thickness of 1/2 cm. Remove the wax sheets and place over the first layer.
- Flatten the semolina dough between two wax sheets then place over the date mixture after removing the wax sheets. The semolina dough should cover the dates completely.
- Sprinkle the sesame seeds on the top of the cake, then cut into squares.
- Bake in a hot oven for 25 minutes or until golden.
- Remove from the oven and pour 1 cup of syrup(*) over the cake and set aside to cool.

Pancake Batter
Atayef

1 cup flour
1 cup water
1/2 teaspoon bicarbonate of soda
3 drops lemon juice
a dash of salt
1 teaspoon yeast dissolved in 2 tablespoons warm water

13 pancakes

- Place the flour and salt in an electric mixer and add the water gradually while mixing.
- Add the dissolved yeast to the above mixture and mix well.
- Cover the batter and set aside in a warm place until double in size. (2 to 3 hours).
- Add the bicarbonate of soda and the lemon juice to the batter just before baking.
- Heat a greased heavy based skillet or frying pan.
- Pour a little batter into the hot skillet so that it forms a circle 10 cm in diameter.
- Cook until golden brown on the underside.
- Lift out and stack.

Walnut and Date Cookies

Ma'amoul bi Jaws wa Tamr

PASTRY
3 lb (1 1/2 kg) semolina
3 cups fine semolina
1 lb (1/2 kg) ghee or butter
1 cup sugar
1/2 cup orange blossom water
1/2 cup rosewater
1 cup water for kneading
2 tablespoons yeast dissolved in 1/2 cup warm water
2 cups powdered sugar, for garnishing
1/2 teaspoon mahlab(*)

WALNUT FILLING
1 lb (1/2 kg) walnuts
1 cup sugar
1/4 cup rosewater

DATE FILLING
1 lb (1/2 kg) seeded dates
4 tablespoons ghee or butter

40/60 dates/walnuts cookies

- ▼ Combine the semolina, fine semolina, mahlab(*) and sugar in a big bowl. Add the ghee and work it with your fingers until the semolina and ghee are almost blended.
- ▼ Sprinkle the orange blossom water and the rosewater and work them with your fingers. Do not knead.
- ▼ Cover the bowl and let stand for 6 hours.
- ▼ Chop the walnuts very finely. Add the sugar and rosewater and mix well. Set aside.
- ▼ Finely chop the dates. Sauté in the ghee over low heat until it becomes very soft.
- ▼ Remove from the heat and set aside to cool.
- ▼ Knead the dates well until they become a well blended ball.
- ▼ Divide the dates into small quantities, depending on the size of the mould used.
- ▼ Dissolve the yeast and set aside for 20 minutes.
- ▼ Add the dissolved yeast and 1 cup of water to the semolina.
- ▼ Work the semolina with the fingers and palms until the semolina becomes a soft pliable dough.
- ▼ Divide the pastry into small balls depending on the special mould used.
- ▼ Place each ball in the palm of the left hand and make a hollow in it by using the index finger of the right hand. Fill with a teaspoon of either the nut or date filling. Pinch it shut.
- ▼ Place the stuffed dough ball into the mould and press lightly to print the design on the pastry.
- ▼ Arrange the cookies on a baking tray and let stand for one hour.
- ▼ Bake in a very hot oven (450°F) for 30 minutes or until golden brown.
- ▼ When the cookies have cooled, sprinkle with the powdered sugar. Serve cold.

Bread Sweet

Aish al Saraya

4 cups sugar
2 cups ground pistachio nuts
1/2 cup orange blossom water
2 lb (1 kg) ashta (home-made cream)
2 lb (1 kg) round loaf of french bread
30 cm diameter

16 persons

- Remove the crust with a sharp knife and divide the round loaf into two equal circles.
- Sprinkle a little water on each circle until moistened but not quite wet.
- Place each moistened circle on a 40 cm diameter tray.
- In a saucepan, place the sugar over medium heat and stir with a wooden spoon until the sugar dissolves and becomes brown in color.
- Pour the brown sugar equally on both circles. Let stand for a while.
- When the sugar cools down, place one tray over low heat and knead the bread with a moistened hand. Shape it into a circle, 1/2 cm thick, remove from the heat and set aside.
- Repeat the same procedure with the other tray.
- Turn out one circle of kneaded bread onto a large serving dish, and sprinkle a little orange blossom water on it. Smooth down with the palm of your hand.
- Place the ashta on this circle of bread in the dish and pat it down with a spoon.
- Turn the other circle of bread on top of the kashta. Sprinkle with a little orange blossom water and smooth down with your palm. Refrigerate for 2-3 hours.
- Serve cold, garnished with the ground pistachio nuts.

String Pastry with Cheese

Knaafeh

3 lb (1 1/2 kg) store-bought, ground string pastry
1 1/2 cups ghee or butter
4 lb (1 1/2 kg) white cheese, unsalted

ATTER (SYRUP)

1 teaspoon lemon juice
1/2 cup orange blossom water
6 cups sugar
2 cups water

- Grease an area of 40 cms on large tray.
- Prepare the syrup(*) using the quantities given.
- Heat the ghee. Place the string pastry in a big pan over medium heat. Sprinkle the hot ghee over the string pastry.
- Work the ghee with your fingers, making sure that the pastry string is thoroughly greased.
- Arrange the greased string pastry in the greased area of the tray. Bake in a very hot oven for 15 minutes or until golden.
- Meanwhile cut the cheese into 1/2 cm thick slices. Soak in water for 5 minutes. Wash and drain, and let dry.
- If the cheese is salted, cut into thin slices and soak in water for 2 hours, changing the water every 15 minutes.
- Arrange the cheese slices over the string pastry.
- Place a very thin layer of string pastry on top of the cheese.
- Place the smaller tray on top of the string pastry thereby covering it completely.
- Turn the knaafeh upside-down, so that the knaafeh is now in the smaller tray. Place the tray over low heat for 15 minutes, turning the tray occasionally.
- Pour a little Atter or syrup onto the knaafeh and serve hot.

Walnut Pancakes

Atayef

3/4 cup ghee or butter
2 cups finely chopped walnuts
1/2 cup sugar
2 tablespoons orange blossom water
2 lb (1k g) medium-sized atayef (pancakes), store-bought

ATTER (SYRUP)
5 cups sugar
1 1/4 cups water
1/2 teaspoon lemon juice
1/4 cup orange blossom water

32 pancakes

- ▼ Mix the sugar, chopped walnuts, and orange blossom water well.
- ▼ Stuff the pancakes with this filling. Fold and pinch the edges together to secure.
- ▼ Brush the pancakes with the ghee or butter. Arrange in a baking pan and bake in a hot oven as directed in Cheese Pancakes.
- ▼ Dip in hot syrup(*) and serve hot.

Date Preserves

Murabba Al balah al zaglouli

2 lb (1 kg) fresh dates
4 cups water
4 1/2 cups sugar
juice of 1 lemon
a few cloves
1 cup almonds, blanched and peeled

1 kg

- Pare the dates and place with the peelings in a heavy stainless steel pan.
- Add the water and simmer over low heat. Bring to the boil and let cook until tender.
- Remove the dates from the water and strain the water into another pan.
- For each cup of water add 3/4 cup of sugar, then add the lemon juice and stir to dissolve.
- To seed the dates, press each date with the fingers at one end and the seed will come out the other end without splitting the date.
- Stuff each date with one almond and one clove.
- Place the pan that contains the sugar syrup over low heat and bring to the boil while stirring. Let boil for 5 minutes.
- Add the dates to the sugar syrup and let boil over low heat for 15 minutes.
- Arrange the dates in the jars and pour the syrup to cover.
- Seal tightly.

Contents

A

All Vegetable Salad 62
All Vegetable Stew 162
Apricot 68
Apricot Jam 255
Apricot Paste with Cornflour 241
Artichokes with Meat 130
Atter 16

B

Baked Eggs in Spinach 104
Baked Fish Steaks 127
Baked Fish with Tahinah 127
Baked Ground Meat in Tahinah Sauce 181
Baked Kibbi 190
Baked Mashed Potatoes 168
Baked Rice Pudding 244
Baked Sardines 126
Baked Spicy Fish 122
Baked Stuffed Eggplants in Tomato Sauce 132
Baked Stuffed Potatoes 164
Baked Vegetable Omelette 105
Baked Vegetables 162
Beef Stock 13
Beetroot and Tahinah Salad 55
Beetroot Salad 54
Boiled Green Peas 207
Biryani Rice 88
Bokhari Rice 89
Bouillabaisse 78
Bouquet Garni 18
Bread Sweet 251
Broiled Spleen 197
Burghul in Tomato Sauce 205
Burghul with Chickpeas 204

C

Cabbage Salad 57
Calfs Feet with Yoghurt 195
Caraway Rice Pudding 243
Carrot and Radish Salad 57
Cauliflower Stew 143
Cheese Pancakes 235
Cheese Pastry Rolls 222
Cheese Triangles 225
Chicken in Tomato Sauce 114
Chicken in Yoghurt 118
Chicken Pie 116
Chicken Soup 82
Chicken Soup with Semolina 84
Chicken Stock 13
Chicken with Green Pepper 112
Chicken with Milk and Rice 110
Chicken with Peas and Rice 111
Chicken with Rice 113
Chicken with Summac 115
Chickpeas in Oil 218
Chickpeas in Yoghurt 217
Chicory Leaves in Oil 31
Chitterlings 176
Cinnamon Tea 73
Colocasia (Taro) with Beef 146
Cooked Rice (1) 92
Cooked Rice (2) 92
Cooked Rice With Vermicelli 93
Couscous 206
Cracked Wheat Soup 76
Cucumber and Tomato Salad 59
Cucumber and Yoghurt Salad 57
Curried Chicken 108
Curried Rice 91

D

Date Preserves 256
Dough Balls in Syrup 232
Dried Bean Patties 34
Dried Fava Beans in Oil 209
Dried Figs with Nuts 254
Dried Okra Stew 160

E

Eggplant Dip With Tahinah 26
Eggplants and Tomatoes in Oil 46
Eggplant Stew 137

F

Fava Bean Stew 207
Fish Balls 120
Fish Sauce 15
Fish Steak 123
Fish Stew 128
Fish with Rice 125
Fresh Fava Beans (Lima Beans) In Oil 37
Fried Baked Eggplants 134
Fried Baked Eggplants in White Sauce 135
Fried Carrots with Rice 90,140
Fried Cauliflower 142
Fried Cauliflower with Rice 142
Fried Eggplants 134
Fried Eggplants with Rice 136
Fried Eggplants with Yoghurt 28
Fried Eggs with Tomatoes 104
Fried Fish 124
Fried Kidneys 52
Fried Liver 201
Fried Meat Fingers 182
Fried Potatoes with Coriander 165
Fried Pumpkin Slices 145
Fried Stuffed Zucchini in Tomato Sauce 154
Fried Stuffed Zucchini in Yoghurt 153

Contents

Fried Stuffed Zucchini with Lemon 153
Fried Vegetable Omelettes 106

G

Garlic Sauce 14
Green Bean Salad 60
Green Bean Stew 157
Green Bean Stew in Tomato Sauce 157
Green Beans in Oil 33
Green Fava Beans with Rice 205
Green Hulled Wheat Stew 208
Green Tea 73
Green Thyme Salad (1) 65
Green Thyme Salad (2) 65
Green Wheat Soup 77
Grilled Eggplants 29
Ground Meat with Boiled Eggs 183

H

Home Made Cream -2- 236
Harissa 11

J

Jew's Mallow with Chicken (1) 148
Jew's Mallow with Chicken (2) 149

K

Kabsah with Meat 198
Karbouzeh 161
Karkadeh 69
Kashta or Home Made Cream -1- 236
Kashta or Home Made Cream -2- 236
Kibbi in Tahinah Sauce 187
Kibbi Shells in Olive Oil 186
Kibbi Shells in Yoghurt 188
Kibbi with Fava Beans 192
Kibbi with Sumac 191
Kidney Bean Salad 60
Kishk 211

L

Lamb Fries 199
Lamb in Yoghurt 193
Lamb Spinal Marrow 47
Lamb Tongue Salad 61
Lentil Soup 83
Lentils and Eggplants in Oil 137
Lentils with Bread 213
Lentils with Onions and Burghul 214
Lentils with Onions and Rice 214
Lentils with Rice 215
Lentils with Swisschard 212
Lima Bean Stew 210
Liquorice Drink 70

M

Mana'eesh Dough 41
Mana'eesh with Kishk 40
Mana'eesh with Cheesse 39
Mashed Potatoes with Burghul (1) 167
Mashed Potatoes with Burghul (2) 167
Mashed Pumpkin with Burghul 144
Mashed Rice Balls with Meat 186
Meat and Pine Nut Pies 230
Meat and Yoghurt Stew 196
Meat Balls with Onions 180
Meat on Skewers 177
Meat Pancakes 227
Meat Pastry Rolls 223
Meat Pie Pastry 229
Meat Pies in Yoghurt 228
Meat Roll with Boiled Eggs 184
Meat Triangles 226
Milk and Pastry Pudding 242
Milk Pudding with Cornflour 238
Milk Pudding with Cornstrach 238
Milk Pudding with Oranges 240
Milk Pudding with Sugar Syrup 239
Minced Green Peppers with Tomato 51
Moughrabiyya 219

O

Okra in oil 42
Okra stew 160
Osso bucco 200

P

Pancake Batter 249
Pancakes with Cream 234
Parsley in Tahinah Sauce 48
Parsley Salad 63
Pea Stew in Tomato Sauce 216
Pea Stew with meat 207
Pine Nut Sauce 15
Plain Rice Pudding 242
Pomegranate Salad 60
Pomegranate Syrup 12
Potato Salad 62
Potato Stew 169
Prawns with Rice 121
Pumkin Dip 32
Pumpkin Soup 80

Q

Quince Preserves 255

R

Raw Kibbi 189
Rice Cooked in Tomato Juice 94
Rice Soup 79

Contents

Rice with Chicken 91
Rice with Chicken and Yoghurt 92
Rice with Minced Meat and Nuts 97
Rice with Raisins and Almonds 95
Roast Leg of Lamb 179

S

Salep 71
Scrambled Eggs with Eggplants 102
Scrambled Eggs with Potatoes 103
Semolina and Date Cake 248
Semolina Cake 247
Shawarma 45
Shrimp and Rice in Tomato Sauce 96
Spaghetti with Chicken and White Sauce 98
Spaghetti with Meat and White Sauce 100
Spaghetti with Tomato Sauce 99
Spaghetti with Yoghurt and Garlic 99
Spicy Chicken 114
Spicy Fish with Coriander 123
Spicy Raw Kibbeh 43
Spinach Soup 81
Spinach Turnovers 224
Spinach with Minced Meat 166
String Pastry with Cheese 252
String Pastry with Pistachio Nuts 254
Stuffed Artichokes 130
Stuffed Cabbage Leaves 158
Stuffed Carrots 139
Stuffed Chicken 109
Stuffed Cucumber 148
Stuffed Eggplants in Oil 27
Stuffed Eggplants with Yoghurt 133
Stuffed Green Peppers in Oil 50
Stuffed Hearts 178
Stuffed Kibbi Shells 185
Stuffed Lamb 174
Stuffed Lamb Shoulder 175
Stuffed Neck of Lamb 194
Stuffed Pickled Eggplants 131
Stuffed Squash with Tomates 150
Stuffed Swisschard Leaves 155
Stuffed Swisschard Leaves in Oil 35
Stuffed Tomatoes and Green Peppers 170
Stuffed Tripe 201
Stuffed Turnips 163
Stuffed Grape Vine Leaves 159
Stuffed Grape Vine Leaves in Oil 36
Stuffed Zucchini in Tomato Sauce 151
Stuffed Zucchini in Yoghurt 152
Stuffing, to prepare 18
Sweet Peppers in Oil 165
Swisschard Stalks in Tahinah Sauce 30
Swisschard Stalks in Yoghurt 56
Swisschard with Blackeyed Beans 44
Swisschard with Fava Beans 138

T

Tahinah Dip 48
Tahinah Dip with Minced Meat 49
Tahinah Suace 16
Tahinah Salad 64
Tamarind Drink 68
Tomato Soup 85
Tomato Stew 171
Truffles With Meat 172
Turkish Coffee 72
Turmeric Cake 246
Turmeric Rice Pudding 245

V, W

Vegetable Stock 13
Walnut and Chilli Dip 141
Walnut and Date Cookies 250
Walnut Pancakes 253
Walnut Pastry 237
Wheat in Sweet Sauce 233
Wheat Soup 76
White Sauce 14
Winter Vegetable Soup 82

Y

Yoghurt, to make 18
Yoghurt, to cook 18
Yoghurt Chicken 117
Yoghurt Drink 72
Yoghurt Soup 82

Z

Zucchini and Yoghurt Salad 58
Zucchini Pulp in Oil 155
Zucchini Stew 156
Zucchini Stew with Yoghurt 156

Piftelutze (chiftele)

1 Carne de gaină
1 Carne de curcan
3 Cartofi răzuiți
1 Ceapă mare răzuită
3 ouă
4 căței de usturoi
~~br~~ pesmet (bread crumbs) 1/2 cup
Sare
piper
boia de ardei
Secretul gustului sau vegeta